EVANGELICALS
AND FOREIGN POLICY

MICHAEL CROMARTIE is a research associate in Protestant studies at the Ethics and Public Policy Center. He received his B.A. degree from Covenant College and his M.A. from American University. He is the editor of *Gaining Ground: New Approaches to Poverty and Dependency* and, with Richard John Neuhaus, *Piety and Politics: Evangelicals and Fundamentalists Confront the World.*

RICHARD JOHN NEUHAUS is the director of the Institute on Religion and Public Life in New York City, the editor-in-chief of *First Things: The Monthly Journal of Religion and Public Life,* and the editor of *Lutheran Forum.* A Lutheran clergyman, he has written and edited twenty books, including *The Catholic Moment: The Paradox of the Church in the Postmodern World* and *The Naked Public Square: Religion and Democracy in America;* the latter volume was named by the *New York Times Book Review* as one of the seven most important religious books published since World War II. His work has been featured in *Time, Newsweek, U.S. News and World Report, Harper's,* and the *New York Times Magazine.*

ALBERTO R. COLL is the Charles H. Stockton Professor of International Law in the Department of Strategy at the United States Naval War College. He was formerly an assistant professor of international politics and law in the Department of Government at Georgetown University. A native of Cuba, he is the author of *The Wisdom of Statecraft* and *The Western Heritage and American Values: Law, Theology, and History.*

DEAN C. CURRY is chairman of the Department of History and Political Science at Messiah College. He is a member of the board of directors of the Peace, Freedom, and Security Studies Program of the National Association of Evangelicals, and an advisory board member of the Institute on Religion and Democracy. He is the co-author, with Myron Augsburger, of *Nuclear Arms: Two Views on World Peace.*

JAMES DAVISON HUNTER is a professor of sociology at the University of Virginia. He is the author of *American Evangelicalism: Conservative Religion and the Quandary of Modernity, Evangelicalism: The Coming Generation,* and *Culture Wars: The Struggle to Define America* (forthcoming). He is the co-author of *Making Sense of Modern Times* and *Cultural Analysis: The Work of Peter Berger, Mary Douglas, Michel Foucault, and Jürgen Habermas.*

EVANGELICALS AND FOREIGN POLICY

Four Perspectives

edited by
Michael Cromartie

ETHICS AND PUBLIC POLICY CENTER

Library of Congress Cataloging-in-Publication Data

Evangelicals and foreign policy : four perspectives / edited by Michael Cromartie.
p.   cm.
Includes bibliographical references.
1. Evangelicalism—United States—History—20th Century.
2. Christianity and international affairs.   3. United States—Foreign relations—1977–1981.   4. United States—Foreign relations—1981–1989.
5. United States—Foreign relations—1989–   .   6. United States—Church history—20th century.   I. Cromartie, Michael.
II. Ethics and Public Policy Center (Washington, D.C.)
BR1642.U5E898   1989   261.8'7'0973—dc20   89–39175 CIP

ISBN 0–89633–139–3 (alk. paper)
ISBN 0–89633–140–7 (pbk. : alk. paper)

Distributed by arrangement with:
University Press of America, Inc.
4720 Boston Way
Lanham, MD 20706

3 Henrietta Street
London WC2E 8LU England

All Ethics and Public Policy Center books are produced on acid-free paper. The paper used in this publication meets the minimum requirements of American National Standard for Information Sciences—Permanence of Paper for Printed Library Materials, ANSI Z39.48–1984.   ∞

Ethics and Public Policy Center
1030 Fifteenth Street N.W.
Washington, D.C. 20005
(202) 682–1200

Contents

Preface

A FTER MANY DECADES of isolation, American evangelicals have plunged into the political arena with enthusiasm. No longer content simply to apply Christian morality to the private sphere, they have become increasingly involved in public debates. Although more attention has been given to their domestic concerns, such as abortion, pornography, and drug abuse, they have also formulated strong views on foreign policy.

A widespread misconception persists that all evangelicals are politically conservative. While a majority of evangelicals voted for Ronald Reagan and George Bush, a significant and vocal minority consider themselves liberal or even radical on many issues. As historian Timothy Smith has written, evangelicals compose a "mosaic or kaleidoscope" that includes a diversity not only of denominations but also of political views.

This brief collection of essays tries to examine evangelical involvement in foreign policy—its history, current context, and dominant trends—in order to stimulate thinking on what the role of evangelicals should be. Those who turn to this volume for specific recommendations on difficult policy questions will be disappointed. Rather, the articles point out the mistakes of the past and the dangers of the present, and offer insights for effectively influencing American foreign policy in the future. The authors—Richard Neuhaus, Alberto Coll, Dean Curry, and James Davison Hunter—are all knowledgeable about the full range of American evangelicalism; they approach the subject from different perspectives but draw complementary conclusions.

Richard John Neuhaus, the director of the Institute on Religion and Public Life in New York City, defends the idea of democratic morality, arguing that it is possible, even imperative, "for biblical believers to contribute to a public philosophy that can sustain the democratic experiment." Democracy, as Neuhaus defines it, includes such principles as "limited government; the clear distinction between state and society; rights of conscience, speech, association, and loyalty that are prior to and not dependent upon the state's acknowledgment of such rights; and the constitutional institutions that protect all of the above." He examines critically the views of leading thinkers who are skeptical about or opposed to the concept of democratic morality and urges evangelical Christians to play a positive role in upholding the democratic experiment.

Alberto R. Coll, a professor of international law at the United States Naval War College, challenges evangelicals to reconsider the rich heritage of Christian realism as it applies to foreign affairs. He proposes ten theses supporting a Christian realist approach and urges evangelicals to cultivate the virtue of prudence as the highest form of morality in foreign policy. Though acknowledging that ambiguities exist, Coll makes a case for prudential decision-making based on broad Christian principles.

Dean Curry, a professor of political science at Messiah College, focuses on three ways evangelicals approach politics and then discusses the implications each of these has for its foreign policy perspectives. These approaches, he suggests, are "attempts to work out a distinctively evangelical public philosophy," based on the belief that there is a uniquely Christian response to specific issues that is rooted in biblical revelation. A content analysis of articles in five prominent evangelical magazines, however, supports Curry's view that there appears to be "no distinctively biblical approach to foreign policy."

James Davison Hunter, a University of Virginia sociologist, evaluates the evangelical potential for shaping American foreign policy. Hunter cites two trends in recent history that have greatly affected contemporary evangelicalism: the transformation of evangelicalism from a position of cultural dominance to one of virtual cultural impotence, and the faltering of American economic, military, and cultural power. Related to this is the widening gulf between the evangelical Right and Left, which Hunter examines through survey data. He concludes with a call for evangelicals to reach some consensus on the religious and moral meaning of America's role in the world. Only then will consensus over specific foreign policy issues be possible; without such consensus, evangelicals risk losing any influence they might have in the foreign policy debate.

Although at one time they engaged in politics only reluctantly, evangelicals are now beginning to realize that questions concerning America's position in the world are of vital importance. Evangelicals can and should contribute to the ongoing debate surrounding the application of ethics to foreign policy issues.

The essays in this volume were originally presented at four conferences sponsored by the Ethics and Public Policy Center in 1987–88. The eminent French lawyer, theologian, and social critic Jacques Ellul has said that the first task of Christians concerned about reconciliation is to "help opposite sides to understand each other, to defuse the explosive issues, to calm passions, in order to lead each side back to a reasonable view of things." At each of these conferences a conscious attempt was made to include a wide variety of people and perspectives from within the evangelical community to help highlight and resolve some of the persistent issues in the debate about foreign policy. The discussion, as might be expected, was at times lively and heated. But it was always civil and enlightening.

We hope that this book will encourage constructive and critical thinking, first, within the American evangelical community, and second, among the wider religious and political communities, concerning our common goal of achieving and defending liberty, justice, and order for all.

MICHAEL CROMARTIE

1

Democratic Morality: A Possibility and an Imperative

Richard John Neuhaus

TWO ARGUMENTS are implied in the title of this essay; they are closely interrelated, even interdependent. The first is that moral discourse and moral judgment are possible in a democratic society. The second is that it is imperative for biblical believers to contribute to a public philosophy that can sustain the democratic experiment. These arguments have a strong bearing upon our understanding of the church's responsibility in a society and a polity such as ours. The implications for evangelical Christians in particular are both disturbing and promising.

By democracy I mean, very generally, the forms and principles embodied, however imperfectly, in the Western liberal democratic tradition. Such forms and principles include, but are not exhausted by: limited government; the clear distinction between state and society; rights of conscience, speech, association, and loyalty that are prior to and not dependent upon the state's acknowledgment of such rights; and the constitutional institutions that protect all of the above. The United States is one historical manifestation of the democratic idea, although it is neither the only nor the definitive one.

The first argument, that democratic moral discourse and judgment are possible, I have made at length elsewhere.[1] Although the two arguments are interrelated, I focus here on the second.

1

Winston Churchill once said that democracy is the worst possible form of government, except for all the others that have been tried. And Reinhold Niebuhr's assertion is familiar to many: "Man's capacity for justice makes democracy possible, but man's inclination to injustice makes democracy necessary." I take these statements to be true, at least within the context of the modern world. We should remain open to the possibility that other forms of government may have been more satisfactory in the past and may be again. We must attend, however, to our historical moment and its future.

I may be going beyond Churchill and Niebuhr when I suggest that biblical people should entertain the possibility that democracy is part of God's intention in world-historical change. This is a tentative suggestion and not a doctrine. It is not revealed but is based upon discernment and prudential judgment in interpreting "the signs of the times" (Matt. 16:3). Nonetheless, it is deserving of careful examination and debate. It may have a powerful bearing upon the public responsibility of Christians in our time.

For a variety of reasons, I find this way of thinking about democracy to be persuasive. First, man is called by God to freedom. The ultimate freedom of perfect union with God surpasses politics and awaits its fulfillment in the End Time. In this present age, the most important form of political justice is what we call freedom of religion or freedom of conscience. In the world today, freedom of religion is relatively secure only in those societies that are or are aspiring to become liberal democracies. Liberal democracy is relatively secure only where conjoined with a largely free-market economy, usually called capitalism. These relationships may not be causal in nature, although that argument can well be made.[2] Obviously, there is a dramatic descent in force and certainty from the theological assertion about God's eschatological call to freedom to practical observations about political economy. But these few words will at least indicate the line of reasoning that leads me to believe there is a moral obligation to affirm, nurture, and advance liberal democracy.

My argument is opposed by a number of ideas and forces.

There are sundry versions of authoritarianism, ranging from residual monarchism to remnants of fascism, syndicalism, and nationalism, plus self-serving dictatorships that make little or no claim to an ideological rationale.

The only global and aggressive opposition to liberal democracy today is Marxism-Leninism, including varieties of "liberation theology" that have nothing but contempt for so-called bourgeois liberties. However, some intellectuals are now saying that Marxism-Leninism is bankrupt and recognized as such by former Marxist-Leninists. Figures such as the "father of liberation theology," Gustavo Gutíerrez, are increasingly critical of the naive "Marxist analysis" that formerly marked that movement. These are promising developments, but we should remember that Western intellectuals have hailed "democratic reforms" in the Soviet Union before, from Lenin's New Economic Plan up to the "thaws" under Malenkov and Khrushchev. A robust and intelligent skepticism about changes in Marxist-Leninist ideology and practice is very much in order. As for liberation theology, the moderating views of Gutíerrez are encouraging, but we have yet to see the form that this second (or third) phase of liberation theology will take.

Here, however, I address myself not to the declared opponents of liberal democracy, but to those who agree with Churchill's proposition while denying the possibility of democratic morality. Such persons suggest that democratic moral discourse and the moral affirmation of democracy are either not possible or not desirable.

OPPONENTS OF DEMOCRATIC MORALITY

Prominent among these thinkers are George Lindbeck of Yale, Alasdair MacIntyre of Vanderbilt, John Howard Yoder of Notre Dame and Stanley Hauerwas of Duke.[3] Though I will focus chiefly on the counter-arguments offered by Hauerwas, in part because he has most publicly and specifically addressed my own position, I include these other scholars to indicate the intellectual ambience of the opposition to democratic morality.

Lindbeck and MacIntyre are robust skeptics. Lindbeck suggests that a specifically Christian contribution to moral discourse in this society is difficult, if not impossible, because ours is a "post-Christian" culture lacking shared points of reference. Christians must be faithful to their "cultural-linguistic tradition," says Lindbeck, in the hope of coexisting peacefully with other traditions, even though lacking a common language about the common good.

MacIntyre's outlook is bleaker. Public moral discourse as such is not possible in a culture that has succumbed to a "modern emotivism" in which every moral claim is regarded as only a reflection of preference or interest. Nietzsche understood our age, says MacIntyre; the barbarians have been ruling us for some time now, and the only thing to do is to cultivate small communities of virtue in the hope that one day a new Saint Benedict will arise to teach us again how to deliberate about the common good. (MacIntyre's recent book, *Whose Justice? Which Rationality?* [University of Notre Dame Press, 1988], implies a somewhat more hopeful future of contention between moral traditions. But the description of our cultural situation in his earlier *After Virtue* has had great influence and has not been retracted by MacIntyre.)

Lindbeck and MacIntyre are profoundly skeptical about a democratic morality. They do not seem opposed to the idea; they simply believe it cannot exist in current circumstances. They may be right. Yoder, on the other hand, seems to believe that democratic morality is possible, but he is emphatic that it should not be pursued. For him, it is not the business of Christians "to do ethics for Caesar." The only business of Christians is to be radically obedient to Jesus. This requires a clean break from the "principalities and powers," especially from all patterns of behavior based upon coercion. For Yoder, as for Hauerwas, an unrelenting pacifism is the litmus test of true discipleship. Both wear the label of "sectarian" as a badge of honor.

Yoder was born into the Mennonite Anabaptist tradition he has embraced, and Hauerwas, a Methodist, frequently describes himself as a "high church Mennonite." Lindbeck and MacIntyre are sectarians in sorrow and by necessity; Yoder and Hauerwas are sectarians by choice. To choose for Jesus is to choose against Caesar, and it makes no difference, at least in principle, whether the Caesar in question is liberal and democratic or despotic and totalitarian. (Hauerwas now shies away from the label "sectarian." His earlier work, however, continues to have wide influence, and he has yet to develop in his usually forceful manner the argument that he is not a sectarian.)

Hauerwas' Christian Critique

In his essay "A Christian Critique of Christian America," Hauerwas traces the way in which American evangelicals and fundamentalists have been won over to the liberal mainline Protestant proposition that Christians should accept responsibility for shaping the culture—much to the consternation of the mainline, as Hauerwas notes. According to Haucrwas, almost all U.S. Christians in one way or another subscribe to the idea of "Christian America." "I find myself outside that tradition," Hauerwas declares. In truth, he may have much more company than he suspects. I count myself among the many Christians, perhaps the majority of Christians in America, who have grave reservations about the idea of "Christian America." America may be spoken of, always cautiously, as a Christian society in terms of historical forces, ideas, and demography. But no society is worthy of the name of Christ, except the church, which is worthy only by virtue of being made worthy through God's grace.

Hauerwas is right to criticize both the older Social Gospel Movement and today's Religious Right for their presumption in trying to "Christianize the social order." But he is wrong to associate that presumption with the argument for democratic morality advanced by myself and others. We cannot claim that American-style democracy is "the form that Christianity should take in history," or that democracy is a "manifestation of the Kingdom of God." But Hauerwas is wrong to attack the church when it acts as a critic in a liberal democracy because he believes "it cannot be more than a friendly critic, since it has a stake in maintaining the basic structure of society." The Christian community, including Stanley Hauerwas, *does* have a stake, though not an absolute stake, in maintaining the basic structure of liberal democracy. The church has existed and will continue to in contexts other than democracy. But a cursory look at the state of the church in non-democratic regimes shows how much it owes to democracy for its freedom and mission. Unlike many others, Hauerwas does not romanticize the church under persecution and oppression. But his writing rarely refers to the everyday reality of societies that are not democratic. Thus, for all of Hauerwas' well-known emphasis upon history and narrative, his discussions of "church" and "world" are somewhat abstract and ahistorical.

Hauerwas correctly wants to avoid the identification of Christianity with any social order short of the coming of the Kingdom. Unfortunately, he exaggerates some dangers while underplaying others. For example, he describes the mainstream American tradition as "caught in the habits of thought and behavior that implicitly or explicitly assume that insofar as America is a democracy she is Christian." I know no one who believes such a proposition. Christians may support democracy because it offers a larger degree of justice and therefore is good for people, including Christians. But that is far from saying that Christianity equals democracy and even farther from saying democracy equals Christianity.

The spiritually fatal, and usually politically fatal, equation of Christianity with a social order is nothing new. Examples abound in two thousand years of Christian history. Eusebius, the "father of church history," came close to making such an equation with Constantinianism; the caesaropapism of Byzantium reappears throughout Russian history, including among the "progressive" priests who identified with the Bolshevik revolution and later those who accepted the Stalinist accommodation that still prevails today; popes from the Middle Ages and up to Vatican Council II thought they understood the meaning of a Christian society; the liberal Social Gospel came very close to bowing the knee to the Divine Trinity of America, democracy, and progress; the "German Christians" blasphemously synthesized Christianity and Nazism; and many liberation theologians have explicitly equated the Gospel with the Marxist class struggle. In the United States today there are Christians on the Right who tend to equate the cause of the Gospel with American power, and there are Christians on the Left who equate the cause of the Gospel with the overthrow of American power. We must always warn against the conflation of Christianity with any social order.

In all these instances, the church failed and fails to assert the transcendent-truth claims by which governments are kept under judgment. Democratic governments recognize that there are higher truths and allegiances. When transcendent reality is excluded from public discourse, the result is what I have described as "the naked public square." The naked public square does not long remain naked; the vacuum is filled by the overweening ambitions of the state, by civil religion, and by belief systems such as secular humanism. The naked public square is created by forces overtly and covertly hostile to Christianity, but also by Christians who, understandably concerned for the integrity of the community of faith, withdraw into ghettos where the "true church" can be protected from the culture.

In his famous typology, H. Richard Niebuhr listed the various relationships between Christ and culture: Christ Against Culture, the Christ of Culture, Christ Above Culture, Christ and Culture in Paradox, Christ the Transformer of Culture. Which is the "right" relationship? I believe the answer is all of the above, and variations on each. Niebuhr called this "the enduring problem" of the church's understanding of itself as being in the world but not of the world. The church never has and never will arrive at a sure and settled formula for being in the world but not of the world. Just when Christians in a particular situation think they have everything settled, the situation changes, and they have to start all over again. We can at best pray for the grace to walk the path of obedience in constant self-examination, uncertain discernment, and forgiveness.

It is this sense of historical tentativeness and particularity, of walking by faith and not by sight, that is so sorely missing when we collapse the complexity of the question into the generalized sectarian framework of Christ Against Culture. We must give priority to the lordship of Christ and to the community that acknowledges it. But in obedience to Christ we must ask about our responsibility for culture—not just culture in general but also our specific historical placement, with its opportunities and problems. This task of discernment is grievously neglected by the sectarian option.

Hauerwas, following Yoder, says the church took the wrong turn when it began to envision itself as a majority in society. Christians then began to ask, "What would happen if everyone did it?," instead of asking, "What if nobody else acted like a Christian and we did?" In short, Christians began "to do ethics for Caesar." Surely there was a great change in thinking as Christianity moved from marginal sect to majority religion, but to claim this was the decisive shift is too convenient a simplification. It would make no substantive difference to my argument were Christians in America only 2 percent of the population rather than, at least professedly, 80 percent or more of the population.

On balance and considering the alternatives, liberal democracy is good for people and good for the church. I believe I would hold that view whether or not I was a Christian. Because I am a Christian, for whom obedience to Christ means love for my neighbor, I want my neighbor to enjoy the blessings of liberal democracy. This in no way denies the fact that, as Christians, we are strangers and aliens in every temporal order and "have here no abiding city" (Heb. 13:14). It is simply a question of doing our duty while in exile. Our guiding counsel is the word of the Lord to Jeremiah: "But seek the welfare of the city where I have sent you into exile, and pray to the Lord on its behalf, for in its welfare you will find your welfare" (Jer. 29:7).

As to love of neighbor, Hauerwas would seem to agree, at least in part: "If we are lucky enough to be in a situation where the ruler's language of justification claims to have the consent of the governed we can use the machinery of democracy for our own and our neighbor's advantage." (It is odd that he speaks of luck, as though democracy were an accident, rather than a divine gift and a rare human achievement.) In a democracy, he says, society is divided between rulers and the ruled; therefore, "from a Christian point of view" democracy is not "different in kind from other forms of states." That it makes no difference whether the rulers are just or unjust, whether they are tyrannical or held accountable, is an astonishing assertion.

In his views on democracy, Hauerwas sometimes goes beyond indifference to what appears to be hostility: "Yet it cannot be concluded that the church has more stake in social orders that seem to maintain in theory a 'limited' state than in those that do not. For no state is more omnivorous in its appetites for our loyalty than one that claims it is protecting our freedom from 'state-control.' ''⁴ It is hard to know what to make of such a statement. Which historical instances would support it? Hauerwas offers none. One can, however, readily imagine the mix of bemusement and outrage with which such an assertion would be met by Christians under Hitler, or in today's Chile, Cuba, or Vietnam. The sectarian oversimplification that invokes a pox upon all governments, beginning with our own, has its attractions. But it is a simplicity purchased by abandoning discernment. More important, it abandons the form of neighbor-love that is expressed in the political effort to seek the welfare of the city of our exile.

Again following Yoder, Hauerwas allows that rulers can be "let into the church," but once in the church they must "act like Christians." Acting like a Christian means, among other things, that the ruler must forswear the use of all coercion. What would be the consequence for a pacifist ruler? Hauerwas responds with remarkable nonchalance: "It might happen that the result would be that his enemies triumph over him, but that often happens to rulers anyway." This line of thinking is interesting in several respects. For all his emphasis upon community, Hauerwas has a strikingly individualistic view of "the ruler." In reality, a ruler is solemnly pledged to keep faith with a political community. The triumph of his enemies is something more than a personal misfortune. But the sectarian has great difficulty with the idea that a Christian can be a member of any community other than the church. Moreover, since every social order of necessity involves coercion, Hauerwas and those who make similar arguments must examine whether Christians can hold political office in any government, democratic or otherwise.

Hauerwas continues: "Christian social ethics, therefore, is not best written from the perspective of the secretary of state or the president, but from those who are subject to such people."[5] One is tempted to ask whether that means Christian ethics can best be written from the perspective of the undersecretary of state or White House chief of staff. More seriously, the question is obviously not one of gradations of authority. For Hauerwas, Christian discipleship seems to require a clean and absolute break from the political order. His argument particularly hampers democracy. Under authoritarian or totalitarian governments the distinction between "ruler" and "ruled" is not blurred by democratic pretensions, and therefore in such situations authentic Christianity is more possible. Hauerwas' common sense tells him that he is "lucky" to live under a democratic government, but his argument leads to the conclusion that undemocratic regimes are better for "true Christianity."

Hauerwas has not, to my knowledge, stated that conclusion explicitly, but others who embrace the sectarian option have. Its most pronounced and consistent statement is by those "radical evangelicals" who proclaim "an ethic for biblical people." The proper Christian posture, they say, is to radically oppose all "the principalities and powers of the present time." They make the seemingly humble claim that we must first and most vigorously criticize our own government. They also hold a romantic view of Christian heroism in situations of real or alleged persecution and oppression. This potent mix of attitudes frequently results in Christians serving as apologists for present and future oppressors.

Such "evenhanded" opposition to all earthly kingdoms and their rulers cannot be bothered with distinctions. Between democratic Britain and Nazi Germany in the 1930s, and between the United States and the Soviet Union today, there exists a "moral equivalence." Whether a government is relatively just or brutally unjust, democratic or despotic, it still employs coercion and competes with Christian loyalty to Christ. It is therefore to be opposed as an instrument of the principalities and powers. The argument is similar to that of the person who condemns equally the fellow who pushed an old lady into the path of an oncoming bus and the fellow who pushed her back onto the sidewalk in the nick of time. "There's not a dime's worth of difference between them," says he; "they both push old ladies around." Hauerwas and Yoder do not subscribe to such simple-mindedness. But I am afraid that their ethical thinking is exploited by those who do, as is evident in the popularity of Yoder in particular among radical evangelicals.

There is much in the sectarian position with which one must sympathize. Surely in a society such as ours, where the difference between Christ and culture is so blurred, the church must constantly be called to recover its own tradition and to act out of its own distinctive imperatives. That is not in question. The question is whether that tradition and those imperatives mandate Christian concern to give moral definition to the culture. Should Christians strive to live in a community of sectarian rigor or seek the uncertain course of obedience as citizens of both the City of God and the City of Man. And should Christians seek to further the welfare of the city by affirming, nurturing, and, inasmuch as we are able, advancing the democratic project?

Hauerwas is rightly worried about the danger of Christian ethics being taken captive by purposes that are not Christian. The irony is that his own ethical thought is more than susceptible to such captivity, though that does not diminish the legitimacy of his concern. In a passage critical of what he mistakenly thought to be the position of Reinhold Niebuhr, he writes, "I felt that any constructive Christian social ethic would have to find a way to recover a church with an integrity of its own rather than simply an institution designed to make 'democracies' work better." (The quotation marks around democracies are worth noting, implying that what we call democracies in fact are not.)

In the search for a Christian ethic that has "an integrity of its own," Hauerwas also develops an animus toward ethical reasoning of a more universal sort. The first article of the creed, that God is Creator of a universe accessible to universal reason, is made obsolete by the second, specifically Christian, article of redemption. And the second article is, in turn, almost eliminated by Hauerwas' emphasis upon the third article, upon sanctification understood in purely moral terms. Hauerwas is suspicious of any ethical agreement that can be reached with those who are outside the Christian community: "For if we know what we ought to do on grounds separate from our religious beliefs, then what are we to make morally of those theological convictions?"[6]

This brings us to a critical factor in Hauerwas' thinking. For him, theology and the church, indeed the whole of Christian existence, fall almost entirely under the category of the ethical. This suggests that, if moral judgments can be grounded in mere human reason, to that extent Christianity is superfluous. In other words, what is the point of being a Christian if one shares the same ethics as those who are not Christians? It is a very good question, *if* the entire point of being Christian is ethical. This is not what the catholic tradition has taught about the church or about being Christian. The three transcendentals—the good, the true, and the beautiful—cannot be collapsed into the good. Hauerwas says that Christianity has frequently short-changed the ethical, and he is right; but the antidote is not to reduce everything solely to ethics. Although it may at first seem an unlikely connection, I believe that Hauerwas' hostility to democracy, or to any other moral project that can be grounded in reason not specifically Christian, finally has to do with his doctrine of the church.

Though Hauerwas has not worked this out in systematic detail, his church is essentially what he calls a "community of virtue." He says he does not want to reduce Christian existence to morality or moralism, but it seems to me that is precisely what he does. "What makes the church the church," he says, "is its faithful manifestation of the peaceable kingdom in the world." What makes the church the church, according to the classic traditions, is grace, the preaching of the Gospel, the administration of the sacraments, the mystery of God's election, and the faith of Christian people. For Hauerwas it seems that the church is constituted by ethical achievement. Even faith, he tells us, is but another word for moral action. The church is the "we" of the saints (or those who are aspiring to become saints) as distinct from the "them." "Justification," he says, "is only another way of talking about sanctification." In Hauerwas' view there seems to be no room for Luther's understanding of *simul iustus et peccator* (at the same time justified and sinner). Asked to define what the church *is,* Hauerwas' well-known response is that "the church is a social ethic."

The point of the foregoing discussion is that, if one understands Christianity exclusively in ethical terms, then one must subscribe to a "strict separationism" between Christ and culture, church and world. Ideas such as natural law or universal reason that combine Christian and non-Christian ethical judgment must then appear as a threat to being Christian. In this light, we can understand Hauerwas' opposition to any attempt to use Christian arguments and common reason in making a moral case for liberal democracy. His animus is not toward liberal democracy as such, since Hauerwas also opposes liberation theology's combination of Christianity and Marxist-Leninist revolution. He wants to be an evenhanded "strict separationist." As we have seen, though, such evenhandedness easily plays into the hands of the opponents of democracy.

Hauerwas opposes any synthesis of Christian ethics and a general political ethics because he views Christianity itself as an alternative politics. It is, in the phrase of Yoder, "the politics of Jesus." Distinctions among the politics of the world are irrelevant; we must oppose them all in the name of the politics of Jesus. The more traditional Christian view is that we must discriminate between the relative goods and evils of the fallen temporal order as the church—a community of saints and sinners defined not by ethical achievement but by supernatural grace—moves toward the genuinely "new politics" to be established only in the coming of the Kingdom. By refusing, as Christians, to make distinctions between relative goods and evils in the present time, we nonetheless make decisions. By rejecting the possibility of a democratic morality, we weaken democracy and strengthen its opponents. More important, we may be neglecting our neighbor and our obligation to Christ, who calls us to our neighbor's service.

THE INFLUENCE ON EVANGELICALS

Hauerwas' and Yoder's views have had repercussions in the evangelical world, as we can see, for example, in Douglas W.

Frank's *Less Than Conquerors: How Evangelicals Entered the Twentieth Century*[7] and a recent essay on political philosophy by Ronald J. Sider of Evangelicals for Social Action (ESA).[8] Frank offers a frequently persuasive critique of earlier patterns of triumphalistic evangelicalism. His main, and mainly justified, complaint is that such a piety and belief are obsessed with power, control, and success, whereas New Testament Christianity is about powerlessness, service, and walking the way of the cross.

But the key problem with Frank's argument—an argument that is representative of evangelicals who are critical of the fatuities and vulgarities of the evangelical world—is that in important ways it is the mirror image of the argument it would counter. As did Billy Sunday, for example, Frank has a largely monistic understanding of what it means to be a Christian in a fallen world. For Sunday the Christian life is unmitigated triumph, for Frank it is unmitigated defeat; one exults in power, the other exults in powerlessness; for one Christianity is all crown, for the other it is all cross. Frank has a truer understanding than Sunday of the Christian's situation in the world, but fortunately we are not forced to choose between monisms. Our situation is more nuanced, more paradoxical, even more dualistic, if you will, than either the Gospel of Power or the Gospel of Powerlessness allows. And this has important implications for our understanding of Christian responsibility for culture, society, and politics.

Frank rejects "the illusion of politics." He quotes Jacques Ellul: "Beyond Jesus, behind him, there is nothing—nothing but lies" (p. 277). The economic order, geopolitics, national security, public virtue—all these are none of the Christian's business. They all belong to what Saint Paul calls the principalities and powers arrayed against the rule of Christ. Ellul's repudiation of the imperiousness of the political in the modern world—and in most of our churches—is refreshing. But the refreshment should be taken in moderation. Indulged, it leads to abandonment of our responsibility to care for the world that is the object of God's creating and preserving love. Culture-formation and politics are among the ways in which we are called to serve our neighbor.

When politics is conceived as a salvific project, it is a lethal illusion. But if it is more modestly understood as the task of preventing injustice and maybe even achieving a modicum of justice, political engagement can be a form of discipleship. Ironically, Frank's rejection of political power and responsibility turns out to be another and very familiar brand of worldly politics. As with other evangelicals who show undiscriminating rage against the principalities and powers, Frank ends up embracing the shopworn agenda of those principalities and powers that are readily locatable on one end of the political spectrum. As surely as some advance a "biblical politics" of the Right, Frank and others advance a biblical politics of the Left. A significant difference is that the political Right admits what it is doing, while those on the Left adamantly assert that they are above and beyond politics. Curiously, they are often to be heard asserting this while simultaneously agitating for their own quite specific political agenda.

Frank's embrace of a Marxist class analysis of America's consumerist, imperialist, and capitalist sins is of only modest interest in this connection. Here he is but repeating received wisdom. More interesting is his polemic against national security concerns, armaments, and so forth, because it is related theologically to his understanding of the powerlessness to which Christians are called. Also of importance is his repeated rejection of the idea that Christians should be concerned about the development of virtue and character. Virtue and character, like power, are illusions and are at the heart of the human pretension that blinds us to the fact that we live by "grace alone."

The political consequences of Frank's putative antipolitics are evident enough. For him, the effort to build or defend a well-ordered political community is worse than illusion, it is idolatry. Frank would undoubtedly insist that he is not anti-American, and that the strictures against the principalities and powers apply equally to, say, the Soviet Union. But if we are to exemplify the radical powerlessness of the Gospel, criticism should begin at home, and we must first oppose American aspirations to security, power, and influence. Of course, those who subscribe to this view make no secret of the fact that they wish they had the power to implement their program of powerlessness.

What evangelicals such as Frank, and the more straightforward preachers of power whom they criticize, exhibit in common is a monistic hunger. Christian Reconstructionism, which is aptly called the liberation theology of the Right, aims to establish the rule of Christ on the basis of biblical law. This is a politicized expression of the Victorious Life and a form of monism, and it is all too commonly encountered in what is called the Religious Right. On the other hand, Douglas Frank, Daniel Berrigan, the late William Stringfellow, and groups such as Sojourners are equally monistic in applying their version of the Christian Gospel in the public square. Monists of the Right and of the Left refuse to accept the necessity of distinguishing (but not separating) the earthly from the heavenly city, the spiritual from the civil order, the community of faith from the body politic, the "now" from the "not yet" of the oncoming Kingdom, the penultimate from the ultimate, the worthlessness of our virture in bargaining with God from the imperative of our virtue in dealing with our neighbor. Those possessed of a monistic hunger cannot live with such tension and paradox; they want to get it all together now, before God has gotten it all together in the consummation of his gracious rule over all things.

The second-century *Epistle to Diognetus* rightly described the situation of Christians in the world: "Though they are residents at home in their own countries, their behavior there is more like that of transients; they take their full part as citizens, but they also submit to anything and everything as if they were aliens. For them, any foreign country is a homeland, and any homeland a foreign country." We are alien citizens. It is not "more Christian" to be an alien, nor is it "more Christian" to be a citizen; both belong to radical discipleship. The preachers of earthly power and control need to be reminded that we are aliens. The preachers of powerlessness and disengagement need to be reminded that we are citizens. When either party forgets that we are alien citizens, the political consequences are disastrous. The spiritual consequences are even more disasterous.

As for Ronald Sider, he has for years been a major proponent of the reawakened sense of social responsibility among American evangelicals. Over those years, he has witnessed and been party to some of the disastrous directions mentioned. Unlike many others, he has clearly pondered the lessons to be drawn from some of the unhappy evangelical experiences with "biblical politics." In his essay "Towards a Political Philosophy," Sider presents the results of his deliberations. He identifies five underlying assumptions that inform his political judgments.

The first and most basic assumption is that "power must be decentralized." This reflects what might be called a Niebuhrian (or, with equal accuracy, Augustinian or Pauline) belief that in a fallen world, concentration of power leads to "totalitarianism and injustice." It is therefore imperative that we decentralize political power, which requires a decentralization of economic power; a system of checks and balances among the administrative, legislative, and judicial branches; and a nurturing of mediating structures such as family, church, media, and education. The second underlying assumption is the need for a "preferential option for the poor." The third is that we must refuse "to play freedom off against economic justice." Fourth, "narrow nationalism" must give way to "a global perspective." Fifth and finally, Christians should affirm the separation of church and state.

Sider's five points may seem unexceptionable to people who have seriously considered these matters, but they represent a welcome advance over much evangelical thinking, including many of the earlier pronouncements of Evangelicals for Social Action. Sider does himself an injustice when he says that his use of "political philosophy" is no more than a "fancy title for a summary of my biases." His statement suggests careful and systematic reflection, which is urgently needed, and not only among evangelicals. Several points, however, need further development. For example, Sider speaks of decentralized political power in terms of "equal power at the ballot box"—"at least in principle." He complains that "the heads of the largest four thousand U.S. corporations have vastly more political power than four thousand ESA members!"

Given the multifarious ways in which democratic discourse and decision-making are actually conducted, Sider's emphasis on the ballot box seems disproportionate. In reality, the president of Harvard, the head of CBS News, and, for that matter, the executive director of ESA, all have "vastly more political power" than thousands of others. Surely the "decentralization" of political power does not mean equality of political power. And economic disparities are far from being the most telling disparities in the actual exercise of power. Many economic giants are content to be political weaklings, while voluntary associations such as Planned Parenthood, the National Rifle Association, Eagle Forum, and the Ralph Nader group have enormous impact. In short, Sider's quick move from political decentralization to economic decentralization is inexplicable, except perhaps as a vestigial sentiment from a "socialist idealism." And cultural inequalities may be at least as important as economic inequalities. Then the question is not whether there are inequalities but whether the inequalities are just or unjust— and by what criteria one would make that determination.

Another problem with Sider's statement relates to the question of globalism and nationalism. Sider writes, "Because everyone in the world is my sister and brother on the basis of creation, and because every single person is so precious that my Savior died for them, I must be a citizen of the world before I am a citizen of a particular country." Few would want to argue with the intention here, but in its present form it could lead to several grave misunderstandings. In the first place, for the Christian, all loyalties are made relative by the judgment of God. Furthermore, the question remains as to where the church fits into Sider's formulation. In addition, the question of discernment persists, namely, the need to discern those orders that exemplify the virtues and ideals that have a claim upon our loyalty (moving the question far beyond unthinking or narrow "nationalism"). Finally, a sensitivity to the sociology of knowledge forces us to be cautious with respect to the dangers of false "global consciousness." A more developed statement of political philosophy would attend to the ways in which loyalty to Burke's "little platoons" trains us in more embracing allegiances and responsibilities. While vaulting statements about global citizenship are well intended, it is generally more productive, and more demanding, to focus on a more modest definition of our social obligations and loyalties. And again, for the Christian, the crucial referents are not nationalism or internationalism but the sovereign God and his saving purposes for the world in Christ and his church.

Toward a New Cultural Synthesis

Frank and Sider represent some of the developments in current evangelical thinking about the kinds of questions raised for us by Lindbeck, MacIntyre, Hauerwas, and Yoder. Needless to say, the questions posed by these four scholars also challenge Christians who do not think of themselves as evangelicals. In response to the proposition that Christians should contribute to a public philosophy supportive of liberal democracy, two of these thinkers suggest it cannot be done and two say it should not be done. Lindbeck and MacIntyre may be right—there may not remain enough of a shared moral sensibility and vocabulary in our culture to sustain public discourse about *the* political question: How ought we to order our life together? Purely in terms of the history of ideas, MacIntyre in particular makes a persuasive case that this is so. But, while ideas have consequences, they are not the only realities. Many forces shape culture, for better and for worse, and frequently in unpredictable directions. For example, the current resurgence of religion in American public life could turn out to be such a force. It might play a part in opening the public square to a fresh deliberation about the nature of the good. On the other hand, it might not. I do not know. But neither, I respectfully note, do Lindbeck and MacIntyre.

We should not give up on the possibility of democratic morality. If it is possible, it is imperative. We should not limit ourselves to our little conversations, whether those conversations be called a cultural-linguistic tradition, communities of virtue, or the true church of biblical radicalism. Admittedly, it is in those little conversations that the greatest truths may be addressed most clearly, but we bear a responsibility for the inclusive conversation that is the culture itself. If we limit ourselves to our little conversations, we simply contribute to the ethical relativism that led some to abandon the public arena in the first place. What MacIntyre calls modern emotivism is still that even if it is his local communities of the moral life that are doing the emoting.

Perhaps we need to go MacIntyre one further and say that we are not awaiting a new Saint Benedict but a new Saint Augustine.[9] It was Augustine, after all, who lived amidst the rubble of a civilization trampled by the barbarians and then thought and believed and prayed and pushed the world toward a new cultural synthesis. His was a situation and a task not entirely unlike our own. If such a new synthesis is possible, I believe that democratic morality will be both a means toward its achievement and a product of its achievement.

2

Christian Realism and Prudence in Foreign Policy: A Challenge to Evangelicals

Alberto R. Coll

E VANGELICALS are at a critical point in their history. After a long slumber, they have awakened to discover that they live in the City of Man and that their citizenship there carries enormous political and moral responsibilities. Having subsisted for decades in the warm waters of political isolationism, they have decided to test the implications of their transcendent allegiances in the turbulent realm of political action and policymaking. Perhaps the best known among them are those, like Jerry Falwell and Pat Robertson, who have allied themselves with the Republican Party and the conservative agenda. But over the long run, the most significant evangelicals may be the radicals who, from within evangelical colleges and social action organizations, are trying to shape the minds of future generations.[1]

These radical evangelicals, who insist that they are neither "right" nor "left" but simply "biblical," are in fact heavily indebted to the predominant intellectual milieu of the Left, and to various currents of neo-pacifism, neo-Marxism, and liberation theology. They are highly critical of the U.S. use of force in places like Grenada, Central America, and the Persian Gulf. They are opposed to nuclear deterrence on moral and theological grounds, and often view arms control as if it were a panacea for our difficult security dilemmas. They tend to place a large share of the blame for the Third World's economic and political problems on international capitalism and on American support for "exploitative" and "unjust" structures. They speak frequently of "peace" and "justice," though not as frequently of "freedom" or "security," and they say little about the moral value of military preparedness in a world beset by wars and rumors of wars. They are as consistent in their political predilections and biases as their better-known brethren on the Right.

This essay does not so much criticize the foreign policy positions that evangelicals have come to adopt in recent years, as challenge them to take notice of an honorable tradition of Christian thinking on politics. They have neglected, and could profit greatly from, the tradition of Christian realism and prudence. Obviously, the radical evangelicals differ among themselves on specific issues. The same is true of the evangelicals of the Right. Instead of pointing at particular persons, or drawing distinctions as to which aspects of the tradition may be most relevant to which group, this essay will simply begin with the ancient admonition: *He who hears, let him hear.*

CHRISTIAN REALISM: TEN THESES

Christian realism is a tradition, a way of thinking about international relations, that stretches back for two millennia. Among its most prominent voices are such diverse figures as Augustine, Aquinas, Luther, Calvin, Pascal, Fénelon, and Reinhold Niebuhr.[2] Christian realism has also looked to the practices of virtuous secular rulers, those whose policies have succeeded in bringing about relative tranquility and justice, as a source of guidance in defining what constitutes a morally wise foreign policy. While it is impossible to capture in a few pages the theoretical richness of Christian realism, the following ten theses will present its salient themes.

Efforts to qualify these themes or to provide opposing counterpoints are welcome. By their nature, theses are not laws or self-contained logical propositions. They are starting points in an open discussion, themes in a universal dialogue spanning millennia. They are reminders or affirmations that open onto a broader, more comprehensive view of reality.

1. *There is a vital distinction between secular and Christian realism.*

Christian realism should not be confused with the secular realism of Hobbes, Machiavelli, Thrasymachus, and the Athenian spokesmen in the Melian dialogue in Thucydides' *Peloponnesian War*.[3] Secular realism, as Leo Strauss has so persuasively argued, is essentially atheistic.[4] The secularist denies the existential and moral implications of a living God who is present in history. Man is alone in this world, his will the source of his morality, and the procurement of his own survival the measure of that morality. For the secular realists, survival is not simply a desirable goal; it is life's highest end on behalf of which the most extreme immorality, justified under the general rubric of *necessity,* is permissible. There is no divine judgment to humble the proud and make the rulers tremble, no natural law implanted by the Creator in our conscience to testify there against the more outrageous forms of evil and brutality.[5] In its worst forms, secular realism sees international relations in a Darwinian light: as a ceaseless struggle for survival in which only fools would dream of introducing questions of morality or limits to the struggle for power.

Christian realists see international relations less rigidly than their secular counterparts.[6] While they are well aware of the chaos, anarchy, and evil in international politics, they recognize that the world remains God's created order and man a creature in God's image. Thus, Christian realists do not believe that "the law of the jungle" is either a description of or prescription for international relations. They are skeptical of the secular realists' efforts to lay down "iron laws" of international relations, the overall tenor of which is to describe international politics as universally and consistently devoid of moral order.

Christian realism sees international relations as more indeterminate and complex, as sharing in both the Fall of Man and in the *imago Dei.* Generally speaking, war and conflict may be endemic, but *particular* wars and conflicts may not be inevitable.

Christian realism places on the statesman the obligation to look for opportunities to turn situations of antagonism into relations of mutual benefit and cooperation.

Christian realism is even prepared to agree with idealists who claim that the maxim "Do unto others as you would have them do unto you" is sometimes a realistic counsel to the statesman.[7] Reciprocity, and the establishment of political and economic processes by which the self-interest of states is mutually served, are avenues through which Christian realists believe that some conflictive situations can be transformed into lasting peaceful relationships. Political discernment, one of the elements of prudence, is critical to understanding when the Golden Rule may be appropriate as a political injunction, and when it is not. The Golden Rule has been successful between post–World War II France and Germany, between Canada and the United States in the last hundred years, and in the 1963 U.S.-Soviet negotiations over a test-ban treaty. It failed in the efforts to appease Hitler in the 1930s, and much earlier in the Aztecs' initial response to Cortez's invasion in 1519, and one doubts that it would have stopped any of numerous other leaders throughout history who were eager to expand their influence and power.[8] If some secular realists go too far in prescribing the law of the jungle as a universally valid principle of statecraft, some idealists exceed the bounds of reasonableness when they overlook the limits to the Golden Rule in international relations.

Unlike many variants of secular realism, Christian realism does not forget that man and his institutions stand under God's judgment. Hence, Christian realism sees war and the instruments of war as unfortunate necessities rather than objects of glory. From the perspective of Christian realism, the statesman should be aware of the dangers of military force becoming an end in itself rather than remaining what it is supposed to be—a limited means to more constructive objectives. Without a higher normative vision to guide and restrain it, the quest for security degenerates into perpetual militarism, interventionism, the waste of human and national resources, and eventually war, exhaustion, and decline.[9]

2. *Christian realism recognizes the immediacy, but not the present fulfillment, of the Kingdom of God.*

For the Christian realists there is an all-important distinction between the Kingdom of God as it shall be realized at the end of time in all its triumphal glory, and the Kingdom of God as its seeds have been planted in the hearts of every believer by Christ's teachings and the work of the Holy Spirit. The Kingdom of God is "at hand."[10] It is near, though not here yet. The Kingdom is near not only in relation to time as viewed from God's perspective. It is also near in the sense that its logic and mores have begun to sprout in the hearts and lives of God's people. This immediacy of the Kingdom has some transformational dimensions insofar as it affects and touches the world in significant, albeit limited, ways.

But the Kingdom's immediacy should not be confused with its imminent realization. Saint James writes of "the kingdom which he has promised to them that love him."[11] To act as if the Kingdom of God has already come may be for an individual a sublime Christian act that, at worst, will result in his martyrdom. But for a nation of millions it can mean annihilation at the hands of its adversaries, together with all the horrors that attend such a fate. It is thus that Christian realists view with apprehension the effort to apply the Sermon on the Mount to the conduct of nation-states.

There is, of course, a deeper wisdom in the Sermon's counsels which, at a general level, can be transmuted profitably into the attitudes of a nation towards foreign policy and into the world-view of its leaders. The exhortations to cultivate poverty of spirit, the exercise of mercy, the pursuit of righteousness, and the practice of peacemaking can have a leavening effect on statecraft so as to moderate the human tendencies towards pride, arrogance, blind selfishness, and stubbornness that are so destructive of a nation's own self-interest.[12] But the attempt to make meekness, non-violence, and a passion for justice the sole guiding norms of foreign policy in a world guided by a radically different logic and set of mores can be disastrous. It can alienate a state from friends and allies, and render it vulnerable to antagonists who will interpret its moral scruples as exploitable weaknesses.

3. *History provides clues to continuities in international relations that Christians ignore at their peril.*

Christian realists take history seriously. They see it as a valuable record of human experience in a broken and sinful world. For them, the study of history is relevant to international politics and statecraft. Christian realists believe that the past is a reliable, albeit not complete, guide to man's future. They also perceive continuities in international politics that, despite changing human conditions, reassert themselves in new forms.

As they peer into the vast and bloody past, Christian realists discern, along with the fruits of the *imago Dei* in man, much that is strongly suggestive of the Fall of Man and its implications for the created order. International politics partakes of the cataclysmic character of human history. It is a realm of indeterminacy, unpredictability, and elementary chaos, resistant to order and rationality. These forces make it exceedingly difficult to construct a peaceful global society.

As did Augustine, Christian realists believe that there is no more persistent trait in international relations than the lust for power.[13] And they believe, together with Lord Acton, that throughout history there has been no more potent check to power than power itself.[14] Hence, Christian realists attach great importance to military preparedness and an equilibrium of power. They are skeptical of those who, in their eagerness to build a more humane international order, forget the elementary requirements for maintaining peace in the present one: a balance of power and diplomacy backed by ample reserves of political will and military and economic strength. They fear that "future-oriented" idealistic and neo-utopian programs for a "new planetary society" blur the critical distinction between the world as it ought to be and the world as it is, and tempt the citizens of democratic societies to neglect their defenses in the erroneous belief that such risk-taking will speed up the coming of a more harmonious age.

4. *The persistence of evil in history suggests the need for skepticism towards approaches that seek to banish violence from world politics.*

Christian realists take evil seriously. They agree with the nineteenth-century Swiss historian Jacob Burckhardt that "at times, evil reigns long as evil on earth," wearing away, though never crushing, the human spirit. They also agree with Burckhardt that "there are absolutely destructive forces [in history] under whose hoof no grass grows," and that "confronted with the picture of the destroyer, as he parades his own and his people's self-seeking through the world, it is good to realize the irresistible might with which evil may at times spread over the world."[15] The causes of international violence do not lie solely in defective domestic political and economic systems (as many liberals and Marxists suggest) nor in the anarchical structure of inter-state relations (as Rousseau and many political scientists after him have argued).[16] They also include the evil and "self-seeking" within man.

Only when we take evil seriously both as a theological problem and a historical phenomenon do we begin to understand the demonic energies of recurrent world-historical figures such as Timur, Napoleon, and Hitler, and the ease with which they surprised and outwitted their complacent contemporaries. Because Christian realists take evil seriously, they do not think that a mere restructuring of the world along more rational, cooperative, and functionalist lines is a sufficient answer to the problem of national security. While they may, and indeed ought to, support such changes in the international system, they have relatively low expectations about the process and the results. Moreover, they are hesitant to reduce current defense efforts for the sake of facilitating such a speculative process.

5. *Christian realism recognizes the tragic dimensions of history and international politics.*

Christian realism takes seriously the various tragic dimensions of human existence and their political manifestations. It sees politics as tainted by man's self-interest and finiteness, and therefore as intrinsically resistant to moral ordering. Choices in foreign policy often amount to choices among lesser evils. The maintenance of public tranquility requires methods, such as capital punishment or war, that would be inappropriate in a Christian's personal life. Good intentions have often produced disastrous policies, and un-Christian statesmen have sometimes achieved results morally preferable to those of their Christian counterparts.

A clue to the tragic character of international politics is the paradoxical relationship of ethics to power. All Christians agree that power should be guided by ethics, and that as a nation's power expands so should its responsibilities. But Christians in the tradition of political realism have also reminded us that the opposite is equally true: the fulfillment of ethical objectives in international relations requires a degree of power, be it economic, political, or military—and preferably a combination of these.[17] Yet, the effort to increase our power so as to fulfill ever higher ethical objectives carries with it the danger of increasing corruption. The alternative is not free of problems: renunciation of power for the sake of maintaining moral purity overlooks the ubiquity of sin and corruption even in the midst of weakness, besides leaving one exposed to adversaries. Power may tend to corrupt, but weakness does not necessarily purify. In fact, as the Cambridge University historian Herbert Butterfield liked to suggest rather impishly, the lack of power corrupts too.[18] Those whose shoulders do not bear the responsibilities of power often indulge in irresponsible judgments. This is as true of civilian "armchair strategists" and worshippers of the military (who are often more hawkish than the military leaders themselves) as it is of prophetic critics of war.

One of the key aspects of tragedy in the political world is the sin of pride—the tendency for a nation, as it prospers and grows powerful, to imagine that there are few limits to its capacity to change the world. Pride, as explicated in traditional biblical doctrine, grows precisely out of the most exalted virtues and abilities. It develops out of beauty, true greatness, and genuine achievement. Satan was the most beautiful of God's angels. The classical Greek counterpart to the Christian notion of sinful pride was *hubris,* the desire to reach beyond one's proper place. Few accounts of the workings of *hubris* in international relations are as poignant as Thucydides' *Peloponnesian War. Hubris* is inevitably linked to tragedy. A nation's effort to soar above the gods has a tragic outcome for both its hapless victims and itself. The alienation and corruption brought about by its own successes are followed by moral confusion, physical exhaustion, and eventually destruction at the hands of another state.

Hence, Christian realism rejects all notions of secular triumphalism. It does not hold, as do many evangelicals of the Right, that there is any nation or politico-economic system chosen by God to fulfill His purposes in history or bring about a golden era for humankind. Nor does Christian realism accept readily the belief that within the boundaries of secular history there will come a day when the lion shall lie down with the lamb. Rather, it sadly contemplates the possibility that, in Reinhold Niebuhr's haunting words, "to the end of history, the peace of the world must be gained by strife."

6. *Christian realists take seriously the world's cultural diversity and the absence of a true global community.*

Christian realists do not minimize the profound religious, cultural, historical, and ethnic differences that divide the world's peoples. Such differences are only partly a reflection of the world's brokenness and man's alienation from his fellow human beings. They also testify to God's provident care, for the different communities into which the world is divided also serve as protective shelters within which human beings pursue diverse ways of life and express their spiritual, artistic, and social creativity.[19] Such differences, therefore, are rooted both in nature and convention; they have the weight of millennia behind them, and cannot be blurred, much less erased, through short-term artificial processes.

Christian realists are skeptical of efforts to ignore or downplay the implications of this extreme multicultural diversity. They realize, for example, that the numerous international agreements on human rights and non-aggression (to which most states routinely subscribe) mask profound disagreements on the meaning of such basic concepts as peace, human rights, law, and morality.[20] Therefore, Christian realists are not as enamored as others are of the potential for international organizations and law to reduce conflict and injustice. They also are less confident that the development of a world economy and the growing supra-national networks will erase the many deep differences in outlook and interests among nations.[21]

In addition, Christian realists watch with apprehension any efforts to romanticize the Third World, to minimize the profound rivalries and ancient hatreds within it, and to pretend that Western colonialism and exploitation are the chief sources of its serious economic and political problems.[22] Such an approach is not only culturally and anthropologically condescending in the extreme, it is the obverse of the rightly lamented "white man's burden" mentality. It is also historically and culturally naive in its failure to examine closely the rich history of Third World peoples, and the uniqueness, dynamism, and tenacity of their clashing cultures.

> 7. *Political morality mediates between the demands of abso-lute love and the harsh realities of a fallen world; it is oriented more towards the carrying out of specific acts than the vindication of general principles.*

Christian realists from Augustine onwards have insisted that the Fall of Man has left the world in a condition of chaos, disorder, violence, and injustice. They also see the development of political institutions devoted to framing some limited order and tranquility out of this chaos as a reflection of God's contin-uing provident care for His creation and of the remnants, how-ever tattered, of the *imago Dei* within man.

One such institution is political morality: the large body of practices, principles, and organizations that attempts to main-tain order within the state and defend it against foreign conquest without undue violence to God's purposes. Christian realists include among the sources of political morality the Old and New Testaments, the statements of Christian political thinkers throughout the ages, and the examples of virtuous secular rulers who, when measured against the dark backdrop of a fallen world, appear to have brought a degree of felicity to their peoples. The just war tradition, Christian and classical notions of prudence, an emphasis on magnanimity in war and peace, the injunctions against hatred of one's enemy (even while one resists that enemy's aggression), and the reminder that all human actions stand under God's solemn judgment—these are some of the elements of political morality that Christian realists traditionally have considered appropriate.

Political morality is specific, action-oriented, and consequentialist. It is specific because it deals not with abstractions, but with particular and often unique moral dilemmas facing individuals. It is action-oriented because it is concerned ultimately with the moral appropriateness, or lack thereof, of specific actions. And it is consequentialist, not because it ignores the rightful place of good intentions in sound moral reasoning, but because it asserts that no political action that triggers unacceptable consequences can be considered truly moral.

The vexing issue of nuclear deterrence illustrates the nature of political morality from the perspective of Christian realism. In general, Christian realists agree that nuclear deterrence is morally problematical because it rests on the threat, and the demonstrated resolve, to destroy millions of innocent people.[23] They also agree that to move away from such a morally perilous situation would be desirable so long as we do not create strategic instabilities that might encourage aggression. What they are not prepared to do is to give up the deterrent unilaterally. As immoral as the threat underlying the deterrent is, it is *less* immoral than the destruction and calamity that would ensue if the West were to engage in unilateral nuclear disarmament. Thus, Christian realists insist that moral reasoning must include within its purview the consequences of particular choices. It does not do to argue that consequences are difficult to foresee, and that therefore they cannot be part of the process of moral reasoning. With regards to nuclear deterrence, man's long and painful history, from the fate of the Carthaginians to that of the Aztecs and Armenians, seems to suggest that unilateral disarmament would leave the West vulnerable to political blackmail and outright aggression by its determined and morally unscrupulous adversaries.[24] In situations such as this, consequences can be reasonably well foreseen.

Christian realists also remind themselves that morality ultimately has to do with specific acts. To uphold principles is important, and to prescribe particular policies in accordance with such principles is also important. But the question that must finally be asked is: Will this particular *action* be ultimately immoral? As *a specific action,* which is more immoral: the threat to destroy millions of innocent human beings, or the acutal death of millions and the loss of freedom for many more as a consequence of unilateral disarmament? Faced with these agonizing alternatives, the Christian realist chooses deterrence, not as a moral good, but as a lesser evil and a temporary expedient.

8. *The virtue of prudence is the highest form of morality in foreign policy.*

A morally sound foreign policy has less to do with moral condemnation than with the thoughtful weighing of goods and evils. This weighing, known in classical Christian political philosophy as prudence, is one that contemporary evangelicals of the Right and the Left tend to downplay. As a form of moral reasoning concerned with accommodating moral goals within the immoral realities of international politics, prudence is suited to a tragic world. Although Aristotle gave it its earliest philosophical articulation,[25] the notion of prudence has strong biblical roots in the books of Proverbs and Ecclesiastes; in Jesus' clear differentiation between the work of the Kingdom of God, which he enjoined, and political activism, about which He was curiously indifferent; and in Saint Paul's repeated acknowledgments of the special character of the political realm, in which rulers were to guide their policies not by a literalist application of the Sermon on the Mount, but through a careful balancing of the demands of justice with the need to maintain order. The indispensability of prudence was recognized by Augustine, by the medieval theologians who considered it the highest of the four cardinal virtues, and by Luther and Calvin.

Prudence, or practical wisdom, is a Christian virtue as well as a process of moral reasoning by which ideals are approximated in an imperfect world. While moral ideals point to the wide spectrum of good ends we should pursue in politics, prudence helps us to choose among competing ends, and suggests means of actually fulfilling them or coming as close as possible.

The first question raised by prudence is: What are the ends, in specific circumstances, that we ought to seek? These ends must be weighed and balanced against one another, and this balancing process may require reducing the scope of some of our ends. As Kenneth W. Thompson has pointed out, "Ethical choice involves arbitrating not only between good and evil but between *rights* and *rights*. . . . In every sector of personal, national, and international life, dilemmas multiply, expressed in the inevitable tension between freedom and order, justice and power, or security and change."[26]

Next, prudence raises the question of means. Sometimes, less than morally good means may be used to accomplish worthwhile ends; in some situations, the ends do justify the means. Thus, a nation may go to war to prevent its enemies from conquering or destroying it, and a politician may make deals with special interest groups to save a good piece of legislation. Of course, the means have to be considered carefully because, beyond a certain point, gross immorality or inhumanity begins to affect the intrinsic moral worth of one's ends. Genocide, treachery, and the mass murder of innocents are so morally repulsive that it is difficult to conceive of ends that would justify them.

The Aristotelian conception of prudence was attractive to Christian theologians seeking to bridge the treacherous gap between the necessities and inner logic of a fallen political world and the transcendent vision of the Gospel. It was Thomas Aquinas who incorporated prudence into the Christian moral universe as the pre-eminent of the four cardinal virtues, and as that virtue without which justice, fortitude, and temperance cannot be achieved: "the perfected ability to make right decisions."[27]

Aquinas accepted the Aristotelian categories of deliberation, good sense or sympathetic understanding, and experience as elements of prudence, and elaborated several others: *memoria, docilitas, solertia,* and *providentia. Memoria* is the capacity for an "honest" or "just" memory, for recollecting our past experiences and those of others realistically, without allowing our own sinful predispositions and subjective desires to warp such recollection. *Docilitas* is a general attitude of openness to the insights of others; it includes a willingness not to close our minds to the infinite variety of surprises that may hurl themselves against our designs, and has a quality of spiritual, emotive, and intellectual flexibility. *Solertia* refers to the ability to act rightly in sudden, unexpected crises. *Providentia* entails the ability to foresee, as clearly as humanly possible, the consequences of our actions and the degree to which the particular action we are about to take will lead to the realization of our goal.[28]

There are important differences between the Christian understanding of prudence and that of the tradition of secular political realism encompassing Thrasymachus, the Athenian spokesmen in the Melian dialogue, Machiavelli's *Prince,* and Hobbes. In this latter tradition, prudence is equated with caution, stealth, and the successful quest for survival at all costs; its guiding norm is the survival of the self or a particular political community, with few, if any, restraints on the range of means allowed for the pursuit of this end. But like Aristotle, who distinguished true prudence from "shallow cleverness," Aquinas contrasted practical wisdom with a series of "false prudences," the most important of which is *astutia* or cunning. The false prudences exalted by the secular realists have at their root the sin of covetousness, an "immoderate straining for all the possessions that man thinks are needed to assure his own importance and status, [and] an anxious senility, desperate self-preservation, and overriding concern for confirmation and security."[29]

Unlike Machiavelli, Aquinas saw moral excellence as a requirement, albeit not a guarantee, of prudence: "It is requisite for prudence, which is right reason about things to be done, that man be well disposed with regard to ends; and this depends on the rectitude of his appetite. Therefore, for prudence there is need of moral virtue, which rectifies the appetite."[30] While rejecting the secular realists, however, Christian prudence does not embrace utopianism. "The decisions of prudence embody the duties enforced on us by things as they are; in these decisions true cognition of reality is perfected for the purpose of realizing the good.''[31]

Within the Christian notion of prudence is an awareness of the personal agony at the heart of decision-making in statecraft. Winston Churchill captured this agony in his history of World War II while recounting the dilemma faced by his adversary Neville Chamberlain during the Munich crisis of September 1938. We know of Churchill's harsh judgment on Chamberlain's decision to yield the Sudetenland to Hitler in order to avoid war. Yet he was a sufficiently great man to admit that

> Those who are prone by temperament and character to seek sharp and clear-cut solutions of difficult and obscure problems, who are ready to fight whenever some challenge comes from a foreign Power, have not always been right. On the other hand, those whose inclination is to bow their heads, to seek patiently and faithfully for peaceful compromise, are not always wrong. On the contrary, in the majority of instances they may be right, not only morally but from a practical standpoint. . . .
> [The duty of ministers] is first so to deal with other nations as to avoid strife and war and to eschew aggression in all its forms, whether for nationalistic or ideological objects. But the safety of the state, the lives and freedom of their own fellow countrymen, to whom they owe their position, make it right and imperative in the last resort . . . that the use of force should not be excluded. . . .
> There is no merit in putting off a war for a year if, when it comes, it is a far worse war or one much harder to win. These are the tormenting dilemmas upon which mankind has throughout its history been so frequently impaled.[32]

Christian prudence recognizes this existential agony and uncertainty and its irreducibly personal context. As Josef Pieper, one of this century's most lucid Thomist commentators has noted:

> The immediate criterion for concrete ethical action is solely the imperative of prudence in the person who has the decision to make. This standard cannot be abstractly construed or even calculated in advance. . . . The imperative of prudence is always and in essence a decision regarding an action to be performed in the "here and now." By their very nature such decisions can be made only by the person confronted with the decision. . . . No one else can assume this

burden. The strict specificity of ethical action is perceptible only to the living experience of the person required to decide. He alone has access to . . . the totality of concrete realities which surround the concrete action, to the "state" of the person himself and the condition of the here and now.[33]

Of all the ambiguities inherent in the Christian notion of prudence, two seem particularly appropiate to our discussion. The first is the difficult relationship between Jesus' "radical gospel," with its seemingly uncompromising transcendent reference point, and the general tenor of prudential decision-making, which tends to revolve around the necessities and limits imposed by this world. Christian thinkers have tried to resolve this tension by writing about two forms of prudence: lower and higher.[34]

The first kind, most evident in the Old Testament and the Pauline letters, has been appropriated by Christian realists of our own day such as Reinhold Niebuhr and Martin Wright via Saint Augustine's distinction between the City of Man and the City of God. In the realm of statecraft, lower prudence focuses on modest goals such as limited order, tranquility, and accommodation. Its conception of international morality is based on skepticism towards any radical designs to transform world politics. Aside from its concern with limited objectives, lower prudence devotes most of its energy to the question of means, to making the inevitable struggle for power among nations less brutal and dehumanizing. Its models include Hugo Grotius's counsels to moderation in *De jure belli ac pacis;* Churchill's refusal to connive in Stalin's proposal to execute 50,000 German technicians and military officers;[35] War Secretary Stimson's successful protest against the suggested use of nuclear bombs on Kyoto, center of Japan's greatest cultural riches;[36] and Reinhold Niebuhr's observation that the highest ethical action one can expect of a state in international relations is an action that is both morally good and beneficial to that state's short-term interests.[37]

Higher prudence, on the other hand, is more willing to take risks for the sake of exploring possibilities open to ethical action. It is, in contemporary Roman Catholic language, "a virtue infused with grace; its measure exceeds that of living merely according to reason—its measure is the mind of Christ; its purpose is not to be respectable but to be a fellow citizen of the saints and a familiar of God. . . . It springs from and lives only in charity, without which one may be shrewd but cannot be prudent."[38] The limits of this higher prudence in the political realm, however, are ambiguous, as are also the boundaries between lower prudence and secular realism. At what point does higher prudence become, in Eric Voegelin's words, a radically irresponsible and unrealizable desire to "immanentize the escathon"?[39] And where is the line that separates lower prudence from a simple desire to protect one's self-interest without causing undue harm to others? More work needs to be done in searching for answers to these questions.

A second ambiguity has to do with the standard by which one ought to measure the consequences of a statesman's actions. Aristotle used Pericles as the paragon of the prudent statesman, in much the same way as some modern historians have done with respect to the nineteenth-century German chancellor Otto von Bismarck. But, judging by the account of Thucydides (a supporter of Pericles) in *The Peloponnesian War,* Pericles urged his countrymen to undertake a war that could have been avoided. The war ultimately destroyed Athens' empire and set in motion its decline and eventual fall. Historians eager to exonerate Pericles have argued that had Pericles not died in the war, he would have pursued a better strategy than his successors and won. Yet, as a prudent man Pericles surely must have known that war is unpredictable. Would not Athens' continued economic expansion, coupled with a cautious, gradualist strategy of weakening its adversaries over the long run, have achieved the objectives Pericles desired without a direct military clash? How are we to evaluate Pericles' practical wisdom?

Similar questions arise in Bismarck's case.[40] Was the fabled master of statecraft a great and prudent statesman, or was he much closer to Aristotle's notion of the shallow, clever man? In his own lifetime, Bismarck dazzled those around him by doing the politically impossible: unifying Germany into a powerful state without the opposition of either Russia or Great Britain, after three relatively bloodless wars with Denmark, Austria, and France. The price, though not obvious to most of his contemporaries,[41] became clearer to a later generation: the militarization of German life, the exaltation of *Macht* (force) in the German ethos, and the destruction of republicanism and regional autonomy, which might have produced a political community far more attuned to the ideals of Goethe and Schiller than the Wilhelmine and Hitlerian empires.[42] We may be hesitant to judge statesmen by consequences that would be extremely difficult for them to foresee, but is it not appropriate to judge them for trends and forces they condone and set in motion in order to bring about their deceptively brilliant achievements? Prudence must be judged not only by short-term results but also by the much more demanding standard of long-term trends and consequences.

Analytical philosophers point to numerous problems and ambiguities in the concept of prudence, extending well beyond those briefly discussed here. Yet, in terms of affecting the practical attitudes a statesman takes towards difficult ethical choices, prudence is valuable in moderating some of the worst errors to which statesmen are prone. The Aristotelian emphasis on self-control, deliberation, sympathetic understanding, the value of experience, and intimate acquaintance with the details of the problem are correctives to *hubris,* mean-spiritedness, self-righteousness, and the politician's tendency to give primacy to ideological abstractions over the more intractable empirical realities at the core of international relations. As discussed earlier, Aquinas brought these Aristotelian concerns into the Christian understanding of prudence, while adding others (see page 33).

For the Christian, prudence is not an autonomous decision-making process cut off from revelation. The values that define the ends of foreign policy stem from broad Christian principles. And the means counseled by prudence are not wholly open-ended. As suggested earlier, certain policy instruments may carry too high a cost.

Faith and conscience are inseparable companions of prudence. In the rough-and-tumble of international politics, faith in a transcendent normative order and acknowledgment of divine judgment may be necessary to sustain the prudent statesman and prevent him from succumbing to the temptations of despair, cynicism, and ruthlessness. The thoughtful Christian statesman also may discover that the moral perplexities of international relations are less likely to drive him into either moral impotence or nihilism if at every step along the road of prudential calculus he lives in that awareness of utter dependence on the Living God which the Bible calls faith. Reinhold Niebuhr had this in mind when he wrote that faith in God's forgiveness makes possible the risk of action.

Finally, there are two popular beliefs about morality and international affairs that Christian prudence challenges. The first of these is the idea that foreign policy can be reconciled with ethics if only a "good and decent man" is placed at the helm. A decent man does not always make a prudent statesman. In order for his desire to do good to ripen into morally sound statecraft, he must cultivate those ways of thinking and acting, those intellectual habits and skills, associated with the concept of prudence. The second conventional notion is that ethical decision-making can be systematized and fully rationalized through some clear hierarchy of moral principles, or a "moral system" such as casuistry or biblical literalism. Here, too, prudence warns against the understandable but morally pernicious yearning for simplification and certainty. Given the uniqueness of every agent and every situation, and the difficulty of balancing competing ends and means, prudence reminds us that at the core of ethical decision-making is a degree of existential agony and darkness indicative of man's finiteness and of his need for a transcendent grace that, in Reinhold Niebuhr's words, may "complete what even the highest human striving must leave incomplete."[43]

9. *Christian realism recognizes the diversity of callings in the realm of international politics.*

An inquiry into the Christian's place in international politics must start by recognizing the diversity of roles that Christians may be called to play. Among the callings appropriate for a Christian are those of prophet, patriot, and policymaker. These categories are not absolutely distinct, but instead describe degrees of emphasis. Every Christian, regardless of how patriotic or deeply immersed in the policymaking process, should retain a sense of alienation from this world, an awareness of how even the most benign and best-intentioned human societies and institutions fall radically short of God's truth, integrity, and justice. Similarly, every Christian, regardless of how prophetic his denunciation of political shortcomings, and regardless of how cosmopolitan his concern for other nations, should retain a feeling of patriotism—an appreciation for the earthly benefits he derives from his country and fellow citizens—and a sense of prudence to prevent his prophetic judgment from degenerating into political irresponsibility.

Prophets have an important place in international politics and in the Christian community. They remind us of the absolute values against which we are to measure our actions. They point to God's judgment and to our utter failure before God's truth. They challenge us and make us uncomfortable. Whenever we fall prey to fatalism and inaction, they prod us to look for creative ways in which, as Christians, we might make a difference in the world of power politics.

Patriots, too, should have an honorable place in the Christian community. They are the millions of Christians who go about their daily lives quietly paying their taxes, upholding law and order, and offering their lives to defend the City of Man against conquest and tyranny. Patriotism is not the same as idolatrous nationalism or chauvinism. The latter represent an inflated pride in one's country coupled with condescension or contempt for other nations and cultures. It has no place in the Christian life. Patriotism, on the other hand, is simple rejoicing in the best traditions and values of one's earthly homeland. It is a virtue rooted in gratitude and fellowship. It recognizes that beyond the tie that binds all Christians in this world, there are other ties that bind us with other believers and unbelievers alike with whom we share a way of life and the obligation to defend it. To reject the value of patriotism in the name of the universal brotherhood of all men is the same as rejecting the love of family as somehow detrimental to the love of God or neighbor. Such ways of thinking may be contemptuous of the structures of the created order to the point of throwing into doubt God's grace and providence.

A place also needs to be made for the Christian policymaker. His task is often much more difficult, and his choices more agonizing, than those of the prophet. The prophet will condemn oppression, injustice, and human rights violations, but it is the policymaker who must take final responsibility for deciding whether a particular foreign government should receive our economic aid and perhaps even our military support. While the prophet can claim comfortably that he opposes equally the immoralities of the Right and those of the Left, it is the policymaker who has to engage in the excruciating prudential calculus of determining whether a particular regime, for all its obvious shortcomings, would be preferable to the available alternatives. From the aloofness of his pulpit or scholarly journal, the prophet can proclaim the beauties of peace and the sinfulness of war. But it was the policymaker who had to decide whether the United States should ally itself with Stalin in order to defeat the Third Reich, and whether to drop an atomic bomb over Hiroshima, killing tens of thousands at one stroke, as an alternative to the probable deaths of over a million Americans and Japanese in a protracted war. While today's prophets bewail the evil of nuclear weapons, policymakers, although agreeing with the prophets over the immorality of nuclear war, have nonetheless to engage in the immoral act of threatening millions of innocent Soviet citizens with sudden destruction, so as to deter their leaders from an attack against Western Europe and the United States.

10. *The drawing of relative moral distinctions, in the midst of our awareness of God's absolute judgment, is a Christian's political responsibility.*

Christians who choose to enter the practical sphere have an obligation to go beyond prophetic judgment to make relative moral distinctions. Deeply aware of God's judgment, they must be prepared to make imperfect, even partly evil choices as an alternative to even greater evils. Moreover, simply standing on the sidelines and "wishing a plague on both houses" is a posture denied to them, as is the option of counseling at the general level as opposed to making specific, concrete decisions.

On this difficult road, as they exercise responsibilities in often tragic contexts, Christians should be ever mindful of their ultimate allegiances, of the divine judgment that transcends all relative political judgments, and of God's embracing mercy. This is a road full of tension and uneasiness, not fit for everyone. It is a path we are to walk truly with "fear and trembling," full of that soberness of spirit and judgment that are antithetical to the partisan enthusiasms with which the political world continually tempts all Christians. Existential humility before the knotty complexities of the political world and openness to God's truth and judgment are equally vital in this pilgrimage.[44] Without the first, the Christian policymaker runs the danger of simplifying real moral dilemmas in order to assuage his conscience. Without the latter, he risks dissolving his inner integrity, losing his soul, for the sake of gaining the world.

3

Biblical Politics and Foreign Policy

Dean C. Curry

ONE OF THE most significant religious and sociological phe-
nomena of the past twenty-five years is the emergence of
theologically conservative Christianity as a cultural force in
America. For over half a century, theologically conservative
Christians—fundamentalists and evangelicals—lived in self-im-
posed exile on the periphery of public life. During this time,
these conservative Christians wandered in a wilderness of cultural irrelevance, believing that this was the price to be paid for
protecting the fundamentals of the faith against the onslaughts
of theological as well as secular modernism.

Fundamentalism and evangelicalism's journey out of the wilderness and into the mainstream of American culture was long
and wrought with intense conflict among conservative Christians
themselves.[1] This story has been told by historians of American
religion, most notably in the penetrating scholarship of George
Marsden. The present essay will not endeavor to recount the fits
and starts that took place as evangelicals struggled to define a
place for themselves in American cultural life. What I want to
emphasize, however, is that along the way most of the evangelical world, including those evangelicals who see themselves as
the direct heirs of fundamentalism, jettisoned a previously sac-
rosanct theological tenet: namely, the imperative of separation.
It is not, I believe, an oversimplification to say that early
twentieth-century fundamentalism occupied itself with saving
souls, period. There was a plethora of cultural quirks—such as

anti-Catholicism and support for prohibition—that embellished fundamentalism, but the core of its theology was about saving souls that otherwise were doomed to eternal damnation.

As evangelicalism redefined its relationship to the broader American culture, a theological redefinition took place. Evangelism remained at the center of evangelical theology, but evangelical theology now broadened to include a cultural or social component. In other words, evangelical theology was no longer defined in strictly vertical terms but included a horizontal component as well.[2] Therefore, evangelicals today, from Moral Majority founder Jerry Falwell to Jim Wallis, editor of the radical evangelical *Sojourners* magazine, see social action or involvement with the broader culture as a faithful response to biblical Christianity. Cultural separatism associated with traditional anabaptism or early twentieth-century fundamentalism is now, for the most part, a historical memory. Apart from relatively obscure, predominantly rural fundamentalist and anabaptist sects, the overwhelming majority of theologically conservative Christians—whether anabaptist, charismatic, evangelical, or fundamentalist—have rejected the strict separationist Christ-against-culture theology in favor of some version of a Christ-the-transformer-of-culture theology (to use H. Richard Niebuhr's typology).

The task of cultural transformation has resulted in evangelicals paying increasing attention to the realm of politics and public policy. The kinds of political issues that evangelicals have concerned themselves with and the nature of evangelical political involvement have been quite diverse. We need only think again of Jerry Falwell and Jim Wallis to realize the diversity among American evangelicals. At the same time, American evangelicals of all political stripes share a common commitment to biblical authority. We cannot understand the sociology or theology of American evangelicalism's engagement of politics apart from this affirmation of the final authority of Scripture. The defining boundary of evangelical theology in general is the authority of the Scripture; it is, ultimately, the heart of theological orthodoxy itself. It is this commitment to the final authority of Scripture, to *sola Scriptura,* that provides *the* distinctiveness of evangelical theology. As a biblical people, evangelicals see themselves as bearing a distinctive message.

This belief has been carried over into the way in which evangelicals of all denominational and ideological persuasions approach politics. Because of their diversity, it is difficult to generalize about the political involvement of evangelical groups. However, three facts stand out: first, evangelicals have become "players" in the American political arena; second, evangelicals see such political involvement as a reflection of biblical faithfulness; third, evangelical politics constitutes a putatively third-way approach—a biblical approach—to public policy. In short, evangelicals believe they have something unique to contribute to the broader public conversation regarding politics.

But in what sense is evangelicalism's engagement of politics biblical? What do evangelicals mean when they speak of Christian—that is, biblical—politics? How is the Bible, which is authoritative in matters of personal faith, also authoritative in matters of politics and public philosophy? Here again generalizations are difficult; nonetheless, I would like to identify three approaches to public philosophy among evangelicals, each claiming to be biblical or Christian. While not all evangelicals fit neatly into one of these approaches, large numbers do. More important, however, influential church and educational elites within the evangelical world have adopted these approaches. Indeed, these three approaches represent *the* dominant ways of thinking about public philosophy among evangelical elites. And these contemporary approaches to biblical politics are built on an epistemology that constitutes a decisive break with the historic Christian understanding of the relationship between general revelation and special revelation.

APPROACHES TO PUBLIC PHILOSOPHY

The first approach to public philosophy is something of a paradox. It is probably the least well known, but it has grown in influence. Christian Reconstructionism, also known as Dominion Theology, is the product of the scholarship of a small group of Reformed Calvinist evangelical theologians and intellectuals.[3]

The core of Reconstructionist theology has been developed by three men: Rousas J. Rushdoony, Gary North, and Greg Bahnsen. Along with a few others, these members of the brain trust of Christian Reconstructionism are pariahs within mainstream evangelical theology. This is largely a result of the highly emotional and even caustic style that characterizes much of their writing and speaking.

While not well known outside of theological circles, Reconstructionist ideas—the product of a truly prodigious output from the pen of Rushdoony and others—have become increasingly influential in the fundamentalist and charismatic wings of American evangelicalism. For example, Pat Robertson and some of his followers have been influenced by the theology of Christian Reconstructionism. Through Robertson and other charismatic evangelicals, bits and pieces—even occasionally big chunks—of Reconstructionist theology have found their way into the theological system and political agenda of the so-called New Right. I do not think it unfair to suggest that fundamentalists have never had a rich tradition of serious theological and philosophical reflection on politics and public philosophy. Hence, Dominion theology—the product of a more intellectually disciplined Reformed tradition—provides a systematic theological and philosophical justification for the New Right's political agenda. I am not suggesting that Christian Reconstructionism has totally coopted the fundamentalist and charismatic movements, but its impact is large and growing.[4]

Christian Reconstructionism itself is built on three pillars: presuppositional apologetics, post-millennialism, and theonomy. In the first instance, Reconstructionist theologians affirm that all truth derives from God and his Word. In the second, their theology is driven by an eschatology that posits that God's kingdom will be triumphally consummated through the work of believers. (The world will get better and it is up to Christians to usher in the completed kingdom. The Reconstructionists reject the idea that the consummation of the kingdom awaits the extrahistorical work of God. To the contrary, they believe it is the Christian's responsibility to bring about the fulfilled kingdom, in all its spiritual, political, social, and economic dimensions.)

Third, Christian Reconstructionism teaches that all human beings and nations are bound by the "biblical law" of the Old Testament. Bound not just in the sense of being bound to the general principles enunciated in the Old Testament (such as the prohibition against adultery), but bound in the sense of literally obeying *all* the specific laws of the Old Testament. Christian Reconstructionism reviles the individualistic pietism that characterizes traditional evangelical theology; for the Reconstructionist, sanctification is accomplished through complete obedience to God's law.

Dominion theology is anything but a two-kingdom view. There is one kingdom, God's kingdom of righteousness, and it is up to Christians to make sure that kingdom triumphs, even if the means used are coercive. In short, Christian Reconstructionism is an inherently political theology. Dominion is political as well as spiritual; the two cannot be separated. Since the Old Testament laws are literally binding on every human being—even the unregenerate—the political sphere must ensure that God's laws are obeyed. If they are not, it is the political sphere's responsibility to exact punishment accordingly.

Christian Reconstructionism's understanding of politics and public philosophy is complex and multifaceted. I shall emphasize three of its aspects. First, Reconstructionist theology believes that the civil and criminal law must be governed by Old Testament law. Second, while Christian Reconstructionism favors a republican form of government, believing it to be most consistent with the Old Testament pattern, Reconstructionist theology rejects the idea of liberal democracy. Dominion theology denies the clear distinction between state and society, posits no inalienable rights of conscience, and rejects the classical liberal justification for limited government, except in the realm of economic relationships. Third, Christian Reconstructionism's understanding of foreign policy derives from the aforementioned premises. The goal of Christian theology is the triumph of God's kingdom, the dominion of God's people over all the nations of the earth. Nevertheless, Reconstructionists generally favor what might be called a conservative foreign policy agenda, that is, a strong, assertive role for the United States in the world. This is necessary until the whole world has been reconstructed.

The second approach to a public philosophy that claims to represent biblical politics is what I will call the Politics of Biblical Justice. This approach finds its most complete expression in the scholarship of James Skillen and those who are associated with the organization he heads, the Association for Public Justice (APJ) in Washington, D.C. The influence of this group extends beyond those who are formally a part of the APJ network. The approach that Skillen and APJ represent has been particularly influential on the campuses of evangelical liberal arts colleges and seminaries. In part, this influence has been filtered through the Christian College Coalition, an association of evangelical liberal arts colleges whose leadership is generally sympathetic to APJ's approach to defining biblical politics.

Like Christian Reconstructionism, the roots of the Politics of Biblical Justice approach are found in Reformed theology. Unlike Christian Reconstructionism, this approach rejects theonomy. According to Skillen, the entire New Testament teaches that

> Christians must not try to establish an earthly state or political community that would be for Christians only or that would be fully open only to those who confess Christian faith. It is not *Christian* justice for Christians to enjoy any political privilege at the expense of non-Christians. Non-Christians must be given every blessing in the political arena that Christians themselves enjoy. Just as the wheat and tares enjoy the same sun, rain, and cultivation, so Christians and non-Christians should enjoy equally the benefits of God's grace given to the field of this world in the present age.[5]

While rejecting theonomy, the Politics of Biblical Justice is inherently transformationalist, though not necessarily triumphalist, in its eschatology. Christian politics flows directly from Christian theology; indeed, politics is a function of theology. Christian politics begins and ends, says Skillen, with "the King of kings and the Lord of lords."[6] The goal of Christian politics is to bring about a *biblically based* transformation of society. In other words, the Bible does have something unique to contribute to politics and public philosophy. In fact, writes Stephen

Monsma, evangelicals must be careful lest their political impact "be bound by their sociology. Evangelicals may end up being conformed to this world merely by reflecting the dominant cultural values and perspectives of the . . . groups out of which they come." If evangelicals fail to avoid this pitfall, "the message evangelicals would bring to the nation's political debates would not really be a Christian message at all but merely a reflection of existing political divisions in our society."[7]

Skillen states the case for a distinctive biblical politics more starkly when he writes that biblical revelation "has no place for 'secular politics' in the sense of a political life that has nothing to do with God's authority and revelation." Politics is not a penultimate human enterprise, but an activity of ultimate importance: "Human politics is not an affair of this age alone; it is not a secularized reality. . . . [It is] one important way of responding to the King who rules both this age and the coming age . . . and, by God's grace, we will be able to carry our [political] deeds right into the coming kingdom."[8] The challenge that evangelicals face, therefore, is "to take the insights of biblical Christianity out into the . . . political world so that their power to have a positive, constructive effect on our society . . . can be unleashed."[9]

The heart of biblical politics is an understanding of justice that, according to Skillen, is built on "principled pluralism." "A just state, a just world is one in which all citizens enjoy the same civil rights and public care." The biblically mandated purpose of the modern state is to provide "nondiscriminatory public justice for citizens of all faiths," while the responsibility of Christians is to work for such communities of public justice. This approach is also sympathetic to liberal democracy, which "grow[s] directly, as a matter of principle, from a biblical view of the meaning of this age between the first and second comings of Christ." This is an important statement, for Skillen believes that Greek, Roman, and Enlightenment political traditions, not the Bible, have been most influential in shaping Western (that is, American) politics. Theologically, this is inadequate, for "Christian political responsibility requires an understanding of public justice and the kind of 'just state' we are seeking. Christian politics is not a matter of *picking up existing means of whatever character* and then using them to try to achieve a variety of . . . goals'' (emphasis added).[10]

In sum, this second approach to biblical politics believes that political justice—public justice—stands at the heart of a distinctively Christian politics. More specifically, this approach is built upon the biblical norm of "patient, gracious, loving justice.'' In light of this norm, a public philosophy of Christian politics must recover "the biblical vision of communal responsibility'' and break away "from [an] individualistic conception of political responsibility.''[11] It is problematic, however, to suggest that this putatively biblical approach translates itself into *distinctively* biblical responses to specific public policy issues.

The third approach to biblical politics is what I call Kingdom Politics. According to Kingdom Politics, in choosing to follow Christ, the Christian turns his back on the "principalities and powers'' of the world. The Christian way of living is a radically different way of living. To the traditional anabaptists, the Kingdom of God had nothing to say to the kingdom of the world; the ethics of God's kingdom were irrelevant to the ethics of the world. Kingdom Politics maintains the strict separation of kingdoms and ethics, but is activist in the sense that it sees its mission as the active transformation of the world. In other words, Christ stands against culture, but has something to say to it.

Kingdom Politics defines justice—meaning economic and social justice—as the *sine qua non* of Christian politics. This theology of politics is derived from a hermeneutic that interprets the biblical story as one of economic and social liberation from earthly injustice. Biblical redemption occurs when Christians stand against the injustices perpetuated by the principalities and powers of the world.

As a descendant, though a mutation, of traditional anabaptism, Kingdom Politics is most closely associated with the theological writings of Stanley Hauerwas and John Howard Yoder. Hauerwas and Yoder, however, are not closely associated with evangelical theology, although Yoder, because of his Mennonite connection, is more familiar to evangelicals. The central theological and political understandings of Kingdom Politics have therefore been filtered through evangelicals such as Ron Sider and Jim Wallis, as well as their respective organizations, Evangelicals for Social Action (ESA) and *Sojourners* magazine. The influence of Kingdom Politics transcends ESA and *Sojourners,* however.

In the past twenty years, Kingdom Politics has proved to be particularly seductive. In recounting his own political journeys, evangelical theologian Clark Pinnock explains why he—like many others—was attracted to the anabaptist hermeneutic: During the late 1960s "there was a resurgence of anabaptist theology and it facilitated the radicalization process by providing theological foundations. When it dawned upon us, we had the feeling of a second conversion. It was Christ-centered and biblicist and so appealed to our evangelical instincts, but it was radical and subversive of every status quo and so confirmed the cultural alienation we felt."[12]

Similarly, Richard Mouw writes that "if Reformed Christians, and their political fellow-travelers among the faithful, are going to emphasize the legitimacy of Christian involvement in political structures, it must be with an anabaptist-type conviction that the Christian disciple must walk in a new and better way."[13]

Standing as it does in opposition to the world's principalities and powers, the political agenda of a biblical people must, according to Kingdom Politics, stand against the injustices that are a part of all earthly political systems. The political challenge facing Christians, writes Hauerwas, "is to be a patient and hopeful people who are able to live truthfully between the times. Only by being such a people will we be able to resist the false choices—such as choosing between America and the Soviet Union—that would have us take sides in a manner that divides Christian people from each other and their true Lord."[14] In the framework of Kingdom Politics, there is nothing unique or valuable about liberal democracy. The only biblical public philosophy is that of the peaceable kingdom, the community of believers. All else falls short of what God demands. For Kingdom Politics the moral equivalence of all political systems de-

rives from theological assumptions, not from a reading of empirical reality.

A DISTINCT PHILOSOPHY?

These three approaches are attempts to work out a distinctively
evangelical public philosophy. Some evangelicals' understanding
of politics deviates from what I have described, but evangelical
political engagement in general is overwhelmingly guided by the
animating assumptions of these three approaches. Each of these
approaches reflects a commitment to forge a biblically faithful
public philosophy. Each shares a similar epistemology which
posits that truth is derived from biblical revelation. Therefore,
each shares a commitment to developing a distinctively biblical
or Christian politics. Each shares the belief that a distinctively
biblical politics stands in contrast to the politics of the world.
And finally, each believes that the future of God's kingdom is
inextricably tied to the affairs of this world.

As American evangelicals have developed putatively biblical
public philosophies, they have concurrently entered the national
debate regarding major public policy issues ranging from abortion to strategic defense. To the public discussion of each of
these issues, evangelicals have sought to bring insights drawn
from their distinctive biblical epistemology. How distinctive has
the evangelical contribution been to this debate? In what manner
is the evangelical engagement different from that of the
broader—non-evangelical—public? How successful have evangelicals been in translating their faith and their politics into a
"third way"? These questions reflect the assumptions that evangelicals make about the source of truth, namely, what the Bible
has to say about specific political issues. Few, if any, evangelicals would reject the proposition that God expects his people to
act fairly, justly, and in a spirit of love and compassion. These
are biblical principles (although, given that evangelicals believe
that man is created in the *imago Dei*, it would seem to follow
that these are principles common—and discernible—to all men,
regenerate as well as unregenerate). But to be more concrete:
What is the biblical approach to strategic defense? What is the

biblical perspective for dealing with South Africa? What is the biblical view of aid to the Nicaraguan contras? Is there a uniquely Christian response to these issues rooted in biblical revelation?

In order to begin to answer the last question, I have undertaken a case study of evangelical positions on contemporary Central American politics.

This study analyzes five influential evangelical magazines—*Fundamentalist Journal, Moody Monthly, Christianity Today,* the *Reformed Journal,* and *Sojourners*—which represent the views of the large majority of American evangelicals. For each magazine I analyzed the content of all articles dealing with Central America in the years 1980–1985. The content of each article was categorized in the following manner: (1) type: descriptive news article or issue analysis article; (2) subject: politics, religion, or interrelationship of politics and religion; (3) geographical focus: Nicaragua, El Salvador, Guatemala, or Central America in general; (4) biblical framework: scriptural referent or general theological referent. The results of my analysis are found in Tables 1–6.

It is not surprising—given the general tenor of the magazine—that *Sojourners* published nearly half of the articles in the

Table 1. The Reformed Journal.

Type		Subject		Focus		Biblical Framework	
News	0	Politics	7	Nic	5	ScripRef	0
Analysis	9	Religion	0	ElSal	0	TheoRef	0
		Pol/Rel	2	Guat	1		
				CentAm	3		

Table 2. Fundamentalist Journal.

Type		Subject		Focus		Biblical Framework	
News	0	Politics	1	Nic	0	ScripRef	0
Analysis	1	Religion	0	ElSal	1	TheoRef	0
		Pol/Rel	0	Guat	0		
				CentAm	0		

Table 3. Sojourners.

Type		Subject		Focus		Biblical Framework	
News	12	Politics	63	Nic	33	ScripRef	3
Analysis	68	Religion	1	ElSal	19	TheoRef	0
		Pol/Rel	16	Guat	7		
				CentAm	21		

Table 4. Moody Monthly.

Type		Subject		Focus		Biblical Framework	
News	12	Politics	3	Nic	3	ScripRef	0
Analysis	0	Religion	2	ElSal	2	TheoRef	0
		Pol/Rel	7	Guat	7		
				CentAm	0		

Table 5. Christianity Today.

Type		Subject		Focus		Biblical Framework	
News	66	Politics	13	Nic	32	ScripRef	0
Analysis	1	Religion	31	ElSal	7	TheoRef	1
		Pol/Rel	23	Guat	18		
				CentAm	10		

Table 6. Totals.

Type		Subject		Focus		Biblical Framework	
News	90	Politics	87	Nic	73	ScripRef	3
Analysis	79	Religion	28	ElSal	29	TheoRef	1
		Pol/Rel	54	Guat	32		
				CentAm	34		

sample dealing with Central America. *Christianity Today* published 40 percent, so that the two magazines combined published almost 90 percent of the articles about Central America. The type of article that each magazine typically published, however, was very different. All but one of *Christianity Today*'s articles were news articles, whereas most of *Sojourners'* were analysis-type articles. It is surprising that the two fundamentalist magazines—*Fundamentalist Journal* and *Moody Monthly*—published a total of only thirteen articles on Central America and only one was of the analysis type. The fact that *Sojourners* published so few straight news articles compared to the other publications illustrates an important trend among religious publications on the Left generally; namely, a tendency to favor editorializing over straight reporting of current events. *Moody Monthly* and the *Fundamentalist Journal*—both associated with the more theologically and politically conservative wing of American evangelicalism—pay little attention to political issues. When they do, as in the case of Central America, their coverage is in the form of straight news reporting, suggesting that the evangelical Left is more interested in propagating a particular political orthodoxy.

Apart from these observations, the second and—for our purposes—more important conclusion that emerges from this data is that only 2 percent of the articles attempted in any way to bring explicitly biblical or theological arguments into the discussion. Of the four articles that use either biblical quotations or biblically based theological arguments, in each instance the attempt was superficial in the sense that none of the articles attempted to construct a systematic argument from the Bible or from biblical doctrine. In summary, there is nothing to distinguish the evangelical articles from what one finds in non-evangelical religious and non-religious periodicals.

This case study is not exhaustive: the data tell us little about the substantive orientation of each article. The study reveals, however, that the ideological perspectives differ greatly from magazine to magazine—reflecting major divisions over priorities, causalities, and prescriptions. While all evangelicals see biblical fidelity as the primary criterion for their engagement of political issues, when they address specific issues—in this case, foreign policy issues—evangelicals seem to be reading different Bibles. Given the wide ideological gulf that separates evangelicals, there are as many versions of the Bible as there are points on the political spectrum. The failure of American evangelicalism to carve out a third-way political option does not represent a failure of their core religious beliefs; rather, it represents a

failure on the part of American evangelical theology to acknowledge the limits of biblical revelation in the realm of politics and
public philosophy. In this, the theology of American evangelicalism is discontinuous with the theological tradition of the
Christian church going back to Augustine.

GOD'S REVELATION

Since early in church history, Christians have debated the nature
and content of God's revelation.[15] How does God reveal himself
to human beings? What is the scope of God's revelation? What
can we know about God and his creation? How do we learn
about God and his creation? These have been the key epistemo-
logical questions that have directly or indirectly preoccupied the
Christian church for two millennia. In response, Christian theology has historically distinguished between two kinds of revelation: special revelation and general revelation. The former is
found in God's Word and is discernible only to those who are
open to its message. As the literal Word of God, the Bible is
God's special revelation to humankind. General revelation, on
the other hand, is mediated through nature, human reason, and
the ordering of history.[16] Since these are part of the experience
of all human beings, general revelation serves as a witness to all
of humanity. The debate within Christian theology has centered
on the limits of general revelation; that is, how much, if anything, can fallen man learn of God and his creation through
general revelation?

Augustine, the father of Western Christian theology, laid the
foundation for all subsequent theological understanding of general revelation by arguing that although man's capacity to know
reality has been limited and distorted by the Fall, man nonetheless has the ability, because of common grace (that is, grace that
is common to all men), to know and understand eternal principles that govern all areas of life. Augustine held a high view of
general revelation although he believed that it was not sufficient
by itself to bring a saving knowledge of God. Like Augustine,
Thomas Aquinas affirmed that knowledge of God and creation
was found in both special and general revelation. Unlike Augus-

tine, however, Aquinas saw reason and faith, and nature and grace, as separate domains independent of each other. Both nature and grace are complete in themselves although grace perfects nature in the sense that grace elevates nature to a higher end. Moreover, reason and revelation involve separate epistemologies—each complete within its realm—but there is no disagreement or contradiction between them.[17]

With the Reformation, faith and special revelation were given a renewed emphasis within Christian theology.[18] Luther believed that all men had a knowledge of God gleaned from general revelation. But Luther emphasized the limits of reason in matters of faith. Luther's warnings about the foolishness and futility of proud, arrogant reason in matters of faith must be balanced by his appreciation for what he called natural reason. Arising out of his two-kingdom theology, Luther saw natural reason— that is, reason which allows mankind to subdue the earth (in the biblical sense of having dominion over the earth)—as an indispensable gift of God. To Luther, faith is essential to knowledge of the heavenly kingdom, while reason is essential to the workings of the earthly kingdom.

John Calvin also taught the importance of general revelation. Calvin's understanding of the relationship between general and special revelation is much closer to Aquinas' than has traditionally been appreciated.[19] While Calvin denied that natural reason is sufficient to know God's truths, he affirmed that such reason, which he calls common grace, is capable of discerning truths revealed in the created order. All truth, Calvin taught, comes from God. In a manner consistent with Augustine, Luther, and even Aquinas, Calvin makes an important distinction between the heavenly and the earthly, the supernatural and the natural, the sacred and the secular.

The tradition of Calvin, Luther, and Augustine represents the historical perspective of the church regarding the nature of, and the relationship between, special and general revelation. That tradition found a formidable challenge in the rationalism of the Enlightenment. The rationalists rejected any notion of special revelation or faith-knowledge: all truth emanates from reason. Ironically, however, it was not only the rationalists who rejected the classical Christian epistemology, but also, as time went on, theologians themselves. Although there were other factors involved, the post-Enlightenment Christian theology that was most closely associated with Calvin and Luther rejected the latter's understanding of special and general revelation. This rejection was in reaction to the rationalism of the secularists as well as the romanticism of theological liberals.[20] Whereas the liberals denied the validity of special revelation and accepted only general revelation, conservative theologians downplayed general revelation, arguing that the Bible is the only source of certain truth.

VAN TIL'S EPISTEMOLOGY

Theologically conservative Christians have turned their back on general revelation in very different ways. Fundamentalism, for example, does not have a tradition of serious theological reflection on reason and revelation. Arguably, the most sophisticated evangelical consideration of this subject is found in Reformed theology. Abraham Kuyper, Herman Dooyeweerd, and Cornelius Van Til are not household names in American evangelicalism. Nonetheless, the Reformed epistemology associated with these three theologians has been influential in the broader evangelical community, particularly to the extent that their theology provides a well thought-out theological justification for a distinctive, biblical approach to culture and, by extension, politics. The presuppositional stance of Cornelius Van Til provides a good example of this influence.

For over forty years Van Til taught apologetics and theology at Westminster Theological Seminary. Only in recent years, primarily through the influence of the Christian Reconstructionists—many of whom were his students—have Van Til's ideas about Christian epistemology been associated with specific attempts to formulate a Christian public philosophy. Christian Reconstructionism has done so directly, while Van Til's epistemology, or the theology that it represents, has influenced others more indirectly.

While an exhaustive discussion of presuppositional apologetics is beyond the scope of this essay, it is important to highlight Van Til's central arguments. According to Van Til, all human beings are "noetically abnormal," by which he means that sin has radically altered the ability of human beings to think truthfully. Human beings need to think because, while knowledge is not salvation, knowledge is inseparable from salvation. Facts—the stuff of knowledge—have no meaning in themselves, but rather they are interpreted according to the presuppositions that humans bring to them. The only true facts are those that are discerned within the context of biblical revelation. "The things of the universe," writes Van Til, "must be interpreted in relation to God. The object of knowledge is not interpreted truly if, though brought into relation with the human mind, it is not also brought into relation with the divine mind. God is the ultimate category of interpretation."[21]

The Christian can know truth because his reasoning is derived from God's knowledge: "Human knowledge must always depend upon divine knowledge. Anything that a human being knows must first have been known by God."[22] The non-Christian, on the other hand, is incapable of knowing truth. In Van Til's words,

> When man became a sinner he made of himself instead of God the ultimate or final reference point. And it is precisely this presupposition, as it controls without exception all forms of non-Christian philosophy, that must be brought into question. If this presupposition is left unquestioned in any field all the facts and arguments presented to the unbeliever will be made over by him according to this pattern. The sinner has cemented colored glasses to his eyes which he cannot remove. And all is yellowed to the jaundiced eye.[23]

For Van Til, therefore, all truth can only come through special revelation. The emphasis here is on the "all"; that is, truth as it bears on personal salvation and truth as it bears on the temporal affairs of mankind. In his sympathetic interpretation of Van Til, Rushdoony emphasizes the unity of truth when he writes that "the facts of Scripture and the facts of nature are *alike* understandable only in terms of the presupposition of the God of Scripture and His infallible Word" (emphasis added).[24] "If we say that the natural man cannot truly know God, then we must

also say that he cannot truly know the flowers of the field." The
bottom line for Van Til: "no God, no knowledge."[25]

In such an epistemology there is no place for Augustine's and
Luther's distinction between the city of God and the city of
man, or Aquinas' distinction between nature and grace, or
Calvin's distinction between heavenly things and earthly things.
General revelation in the way that it has been historically defined
is an unacceptable—that is, a theologically unorthodox—form
of syncretism. Christian thought, Rushdoony warns, "has consistently gone astray, throughout most of its history, by seeking
to answer the world in terms of the world's own categories."
The specific danger of an autonomous understanding of general
revelation is spelled out by Van Til: "If one fact can be known
without reference to God there is no good reason not to hold
that all facts can be known without reference to God. When the
elephant of naturalism once has his nose in the door, he will not
be satisfied until he is all the way in."[26]

Of course, Van Til's epistemology is more complex than I
have described it in this brief summary. His theology, for
example, does allow for a doctrine of common grace. Nonetheless, I believe that I have accurately described Van Til's central
understanding of the relationship between general revelation and
special revelation, which is that the former is ultimately dependent on the later.

However, critics not sympathetic to Van Til might complain
that I have imputed an epistemology to American evangelicalism
that is held only by a minority of evangelicals. I want to emphasize again that Van Til's ideas are not well known outside of the
Reformed–Christian Reconstructionist nexus; nevertheless, the
general thrust of his epistemology is shared by vast numbers of
evangelicals, including those who adhere to the three approaches to politics I discussed above. American evangelicals
define their political involvement by reference to their biblical
fidelity. It is the central thesis of this essay that this evangelical
understanding of politics constitutes a break with the historical
Christian understanding of biblical epistemology. All of this
would not matter much if these issues simply represented an

arcane intramural theological squabble. The stakes, however, are much higher.

EDUCATING WORLD CITIZENS

The rebirth of an evangelical political conscience is a welcome addition to the marketplace of ideas that is American democracy. Evangelicals have viewed their new role as one of bringing a fresh and unique perspective to the public square. Most evangelicals would reject the suggestion that this effort has been tainted by extra-biblical considerations. If this suggestion were true, the foundation upon which American evangelicalism's re-entry into American cultural life has been built would be undermined. And yet, as my earlier case study suggests, for all its genuine commitment to a distinctively biblical third way, specific evangelical engagement of politics is in fact grounded in extra-biblical considerations. There is simply no evidence that the evangelical engagement of politics is substantially different from that of other groups.

The dangers inherent in the contemporary evangelical engagement of foreign policy issues are clearly illustrated by recent events on evangelical college campuses. The past three years have seen an intense effort on the part of the Christian College Consortium—an association of the leading evangelical liberal arts colleges—to restructure their curricula in order to make them more "internationalized." Indeed, "internationalizing the curriculum" has been *the* priority item on the academic agenda of the leading evangelical colleges since 1986. Why this relatively recent interest in global education?

The answer is to be found in a new theological affirmation that has become popular among evangelical educators; namely, that as Christians we are "world citizens." Christian discipleship, we are told, requires that Christians understand that their loyalties are transnational. In a recent letter to all Christian College Consortium faculty, a Trinity College dean writes that "many concerns relating to global awareness are shared across all sectors of [American] higher education. However, Christian colleges are *distinguished* from their secular counterparts by a theological motivation for preparing world citizens."

There is a real sense, of course, in which Christians are members of a transnational movement; hence the slogan "world Christian" is not theologically meaningless. But I wish to highlight the manner in which evangelical college administrators and faculty have embraced this idea. What is it that, in the words of the Trinity dean, distinguishes the evangelical approach to global awareness? We get a instructive glimpse when we examine the proceedings of the 1986 Faith/Learning Institute, which launched the Christian College Consortium's "internationalizing the curriculum" program. At this conference, ostensibly devoted to the clarification of curricular goals, there were no fewer than seven public attacks against the then-recent U.S. bombing raid on Libya. These attacks were not delivered as parenthetical asides, but rather were clearly seen by many of the participants as consistent with a distinctively biblical approach to global education. More specifically, these pronouncements were viewed as prophetic condemnations and thus as consistent with evangelical higher education's mission of educating world citizens.

The subsequent evolution of global education on evangelical campuses demonstrates that many—though not all—evangelical educators interpret their distinctively biblical mandate as requiring blanket condemnations of capitalism, U.S. foreign policy, and middle-class values. Moreover, this global awareness means teaching that the United States is an ethnocentric, imperialist nation that allies itself with forces on the wrong side of history. True world citizenship requires that Christians embrace just, revolutionary societies such as Cuba and Nicaragua. Is this analysis overstated? I think not. One central conclusion emerges: under the guise of being distinctively biblical—under the guise of world citizenship—evangelical colleges may be developing approaches to international education that are rooted in assumptions about American society, Western culture, and international politics that are unequivocally extra-biblical.

As suggested in my case study, however, and in the scholarship of others, there is no distinctively biblical approach to foreign policy. Should the United States support sanctions against South Africa or not? Should we listen to Bishop Tutu or Chief Buthelezi? Should the United States fund the contras? How should we approach the Sandinistas? Should we deploy a full-blown strategic defense system, a modified system, or no system at all? How should the United States respond to the initiatives of Mikhail Gorbachev? What is the nature of earthly peace? What is the relationship among peace, justice, and the various political systems? How can poverty and gross material inequities be reduced?

These are questions that can only be answered in the context of a careful reading of history, a keen understanding of political philosophy, and a thorough acquaintance with the empirical evidence. Evangelicals differ on each of these issues and I suspect this will always be the case. What is troublesome is not that evangelicals differ, but that they approach these issues as if they can find a distinctively biblical answer to each of them. In doing this, evangelicals confuse the earthly with the heavenly, and in the process produce bad politics as well as bad theology.

The impact that evangelicals make on public philosophy will first of all depend on their ability and willingness to throw off the insecurities that were an understandable part of their early heritage. They need to reclaim the tradition of Augustine, Aquinas, Luther, and Calvin, a tradition which understood that, ultimately, the affairs of this world are not coextensive with the Kingdom of God. Evangelicals must also acknowledge that biblical faithfulness demands above all else that they stand as uncompromising witnesses to transcendent truth. In other words, evangelicals will be true to their orthodox theological heritage and will make their most important contribution to public philosophy to the extent that they stand as a witness to the limits of politics. As the Dutch theologian H. M. Kuitert reminds us, the dead are not raised through politics; there is no political road to the Kingdom of God.

Nonetheless, politics is important. Earthly peace and justice cannot be discussed in a political vacuum. American evangelicalism's infatuation with a distinctive third way constitutes a negation of politics by insisting that we can somehow rise above the politics of this world. No political ideology or political system is acceptable if it falls short of eschatological perfection. In espousing such ideas, evangelical theology, for whatever reason, has lost sight of the central doctrine of Christianity, namely, the pervasive nature of sin. Evangelicals differ in their eschatological interpretations, but none of the historic interpretations lead inevitably to the kind of triumphalism implicit (and explicit) in much of American evangelicalism's recent engagement of politics. Throughout history Christianity has affirmed the paradox of the Christian's life: we are in the world but not of the world; we are citizens of both Jerusalem and Athens. In the telling words of H. Richard Niebuhr, we live in the "meanwhile," knowing our true home, but also knowing that biblical faithfulness demands we act responsibly, that is, prudently, in our adopted home.

In this world, we must acknowledge, as did Augustine and Luther, that life is morally ambiguous. The choices that confront us regarding politics, especially foreign policy choices, are often less than perfect. We cannot choose absolute peace or absolute justice, for these do not exist in the meanwhile. In short, there is no third way. We can say there is and we can act as if there were, but to do so is bad theory and worse practice. All earthly politics, and there is no other kind in the here and now, involves prudential judgments, and such judgments must inevitably be made through the appeal to general revelation. The great political issues of our time, issues of war and tyranny, can be addressed through no other route.

In summary, unless evangelicals learn to speak the language of general revelation they will find themselves increasingly on the margins of serious foreign policy discussion in this country. Indeed, it is ironic that having re-entered the cultural mainstream of American life, evangelicals, by their own actions, are endangering their ability to speak meaningfully and responsibly to that culture.

4

The Shaping of American Foreign Policy

James Davison Hunter

O N THE FACE of it, the idea that there is a close connection between evangelical Christianity and the complex world of foreign policy seems strained if not ludicrous. What possible relevance could this particular form of Protestantism have to the complex relations between nations? Who, among State Department minions, could possibly care what *Sojourners* or *Christianity Today* thinks about, say, U.S. policy in Latin America or in South Central Asia? Though evangelicalism may seem irrelevant to the shaping of foreign policy, foreign policy is anything but irrelevant to evangelicalism, however. Indeed, it has been an evangelical passion for quite some time.

For evangelicals, foreign policy is relevant mainly at two levels. At an abstract level, how can evangelicals contribute to setting the moral boundaries of foreign policy debate? At a practical level, what pressure can evangelicals bring to bear on particular issues that involve the interests, values, and commitments of the larger religious and moral community? At both levels, evangelicals have a stake (or believe they do) in the outcome.

I will not attempt to make a single, partisan argument about evangelicals and foreign policy. I will, however, explore the general relationship as a prologue to a more partisan discussion. My goal is to provide a frame of reference that will stimulate theological or philosophical reflection about the role that evangelicalism *should* play in shaping American foreign policy.

To set out that frame of reference I will pursue two specific objectives. One of these is to explore the ways in which evangelicals currently approach foreign policy issues—not in the abstract discourse of political philosophy, but in the grammar of sociological pragmatism, that is, the concrete ways in which evangelicals express foreign policy interests in the public sphere. A second objective will be to explore the potential that evangelical Christians have for shaping the policy debate. It is best, however, not to immediately tackle these objectives, since the empirical relationship between evangelicalism and American foreign policy exists within a larger historical and cultural context. Defining that context is a task that is broad in scope but relevant in practical ways.

EVANGELICALISM AND AMERICA IN THE MODERN WORLD

The task can be broken into two parts. The first concerns the fate of evangelical Christianity in twentieth-century America; the second concerns the fate of America in the modern world. The former is the story of evangelicalism's transformation from a position of cultural dominance to cultural impotence.

The dominance of reformational Christianity in American culture can be understood in a variety of ways. The first and most obvious way is in the development and expansion of the modern economic enterprise. The well-known German social scientist Max Weber argued at the beginning of this century that a popular variant of reformational theology provided the psychological basis for the highly rationalized, commercial, and entrepreneurial capitalism that came to dominate the Western world. His argument is one of the most famous in the history of modern social science and one of the most controversial. Whether one accepts the argument in detail, one can accept the general association between Protestantism and modern capitalism.

Protestantism may have been necessary to the rise of rational capitalism in Europe or the historical link may have been accidental. The Protestant ethic may have spawned the modern economic enterprise or merely intensified and extended tendencies already present. Either way, Protestantism was linked to a large extent with the forces favorable to commercial capitalism. Though different countries came to the fore at different times, the Protestant powers generally maintained economic and political hegemony from the seventeenth through the nineteenth century.

Protestants dominated economic expansion in North America as well. The Puritan ethos of hard work, sobriety, frugality, and restraint was institutionalized in the family—the predominant social organization in the United States up to the early decades of this century. The families and churches of small-town America provided a stimulus and legitimation for economic growth, first in an agrarian, mercantile, artisan economy and later in a budding industrial and commercial economy.

All this is only one of the ways in which Protestantism can be thought of as having had cultural hegemony. In America especially, its hegemony was far more extensive. From the colonial period to the middle of the nineteenth century, America was almost entirely Protestant. In 1790, Catholics were 1 percent of the American population, Jews an even smaller number. While most Americans were not formal members of a denomination, the overwhelming majority were Protestant in either background or conviction. The ethos of everyday life was Protestant.

The churches also exerted political authority in the years prior to the founding of the republic; afterward, they continued to provide both religious and moral authority. The majority of Protestants, even as late as the mid-nineteenth century, were willing to trust the state to educate children. As Timothy Smith has shown, Protestants of all denominations were "confident that education would be 'religious' still. The sects identified their common beliefs with those of the nation, their mission with America's mission."[1]

This mystic vision of a Christian America—of a "redeemer nation," as Ernest Lee Tuveson put it, probably shows the cultural hegemony of Protestantism better than anything else. Protestant activity derived both inspiration and direction from this vision for more than three centuries. There was unity in this activity in spite of doctrinal and liturgical differences.

Thus to Protestants, particularly in the eighteenth and nineteenth centuries, their cultural dominance and their role in the expansion of the modern world order were not at all coincidental. They viewed their dominance as the expression of the superiority of true religion. Christianity was the "religion of the dominant nations of the earth." At the end of the nineteenth century, the dominant evangelical vision equated the expansion of Christianity with the expansion of Protestant countries, and in particular, the United States. America, as a Christian nation, would assume a special position in the unfolding of history.

Though the United States dominated the world order by the early decades of the twentieth century, the promise of the millennium failed. First in Europe and then in the United States, the Protestant cultural system lost influence. To the degree that it continued to be associated with dominant powers of society, it did so only in a diffused way—as an opaque religion of the republic. In this form it continued to legitimate market exchanges, industrial development, and colonial expansion. Nonetheless, as concrete religion, it rapidly became less important to incentive and duty in the workplace.

The modern world achieved practical autonomy from a cultural system that had favored its development. All this lies well beyond argument. It is curious that the culture of evangelical Protestantism retained its status as a public ideology in America right through the end of the nineteenth century. It gripped the public imagination of America to an extent unknown in Great Britain or on the continent. Its theology, while taken seriously by only a minority at this time, still carried cultural respectability. The same can be said for its definitions of moral propriety, familial relations and responsibilities, and the place and significance of the self.

The collapse of the cultural hegemony of Protestantism has taken place in two principal stages. The "first disestablishment" occurred from roughly 1890 to 1925 and was primarily theological. The issues concerned the Scriptures, the origins of the world, miracles, and salvation. The "second disestablishment" has involved the decline of the moral and familial traditions of Protestantism. The trend started in the late nineteenth century, but not until the 1960s did it gain serious momentum. Such issues as sexuality (homosexuality/heterosexuality), authority in the family, family roles, the sanctity of human life, public education, and the like have provided the terrain for this disestablishment.

Experimentation in lifestyles (from open marriages to homosexual marriages to co-habitation outside of marriage), in drugs, and in religious experience (from human potential cults to Eastern mysticism) provided an internal challenge; the Equal Rights Amendment, the Gay Rights initiative, and changes in abortion and school prayer laws provided an external challenge. These challenges fostered a significant backlash among conservative Protestants, who have tried to stem the tide. Even so, the second stage in the decline is essentially an accomplished fact.

A Faltering Hegemony

Understanding this decline is the first step toward grasping the present role of evangelicalism in foreign affairs. Another contextual factor I want to note concerns the fate of America in the modern world. This too is a story of a transformation, from decisive hegemony to an economic, military, and cultural faltering.

America's rise to power accompanied its entry into World War I. United States military power not only hastened the end of the war, it symbolized expanding U.S. influence around the world. This influence was also economic, with the merger of various autonomous (often family-controlled) firms into the trusts, cartels, and corporations of monopoly capitalism. The United States became the economic leader of the world from 1945 to the early 1970s. A "pax Americana" characterized this period in much the same way as a "pax Britannica" characterized international affairs in the nineteenth century.

American domination, however, began to falter seriously in the early 1970s, especially in military terms. Arms-limitation and test-ban treaties were not necessary in the 1940s and 1950s when the United States thoroughly dominated nuclear technology and deployment. As that lead narrowed in the 1960s and 1970s, "détente" with the Soviet Union seemed prudent. The present "urgency" felt by large portions of the populace and leadership to achieve a stable treaty with the Soviets reflects the fact of a rough nuclear parity.

Military decline is also visible in the demand for U.S. allies to bear a greater share of defense. In the late 1970s, the Japanese began to think again about rearmament and they have accordingly increased expenditures, though only marginally thus far. Much the same could be said about Western Europe. From the 1970s to the present, the United States has been pressing the NATO countries to expand their defense budgets and to station nuclear weapons on their soil.

Another hint of faltering military hegemony emerges from the variations in expenditures on major weapon systems exported to the Third World. In 1960, the United States accounted for nearly half of the world expenditures, dwarfing all other countries. Britain exported 16 percent and the Soviet Union 14 percent. From 1965 to 1975, the United Stages and the Soviet Union maintained a rough parity, each accounting for roughly one-third of the world total.[2]

Beyond these numerical signs of military decline, however, lies an important symbol—the American exodus from Vietnam—the first war in history that America lost.

Another aspect of faltering American hegemony is in economics, particularly in changes in per capita gross national product. By the early 1980s, the United States had fallen to tenth among all nations in this category, ranking behind almost every country in Northern Europe except the United Kingdom. Telling trends have also emerged in world trade. Between 1948 and 1972, Japan went from exporting 2 percent of what the United States exported to 58 percent. During the same period, the countries of the European Common Market went from exporting half as much as the United States to exporting just under three times as much. U.S. trade remains virtually as high as that of any individual country, but its competitive lead has dwindled sharply. A similar pattern exists in leadership in industrial production. In 1956, forty-two of the largest fifty corporations in the world were American owned and run. By 1980 this number had dropped to twenty-three. The most dramatic decline took place after 1970. The number of firms located in the countries of the Common Market increased from eight to twenty in these years, but the sharpest increase occurred in Japan, and to a lesser extent in the Third World. The United States has given up leadership in petroleum, automobile manufacturing, chemicals, electrical equipment, and steel and iron production.[3]

American capitalism is not failing. Indeed, there are many signs of its vitality. But the revitalization of capitalism in the Common Market through the privatization of industry and the growing vitality of private enterprise in the Third World and East Asia have intensified global economic competition.

Further faltering can be found in the diplomatic sphere. The United States has accumulated a long record of successes and failures in the twentieth century. But the post-Vietnam era has been fraught with unresolved crises in Cambodia, Afghanistan, Iran, Nicaragua, and South Africa.

Many social scientists believe that America's position in the world is not unlike that of Britain a century ago, or of the United Provinces (today's Netherlands) in the mid-to-late-seventeenth century. Their hegemonies eroded in the face of an increasingly competitive world political economy. Just as Britain lost strength to expanding German and American interests, so the United States is faltering due to increasing competition from Asian-Pacific nations, particularly Japan, and the Common Market. And as Britain failed to make the transition from an economy based on family-owned firms to one based on corporate conglomerates, so the United States may fail to adapt to new forms of economic organization that further concentrate capital.

There are limits to the analogy, and the process is not inevitable. Yet parallels are striking. American military, economic, and political domination in the world is simply not all that it used to be.

The Foreign Policy Debate

At the risk of oversimplifying, I would argue that *much of the foreign policy debate is framed by the question of what to do about America's faltering hegemony in the world.*

At one end of the continuum, isolationists, at least since the early 1970s, have often viewed American hegemony as violent and exploitative. The United States has no right to interfere in the internal affairs of a nation (whether Vietnam, Grenada, Nicaragua, or El Salvador). Neither can it justify a large military presence on foreign territory beyond what is needed to maintain legitimate national interests (say in Panama, Greece, or the Philippines). America is not the *gendarme du monde,* called on to curb Soviet expansionism; Libyan, Iranian, or Syrian belligerence; or international terrorism.

At the other end of the spectrum, a thoroughgoing interventionism assumes that American hegemony is basically good; the United States has a legitimate claim, if not the obligation, to assert its economic and military authority around the world. For all our imperfections, the world is a better place because of our efforts. We must maintain hegemony at all costs because America may well hold out the only possibility of a relatively just global order.

Evangelicalism and Foreign Policy

What does all this have to do with contemporary evangelicalism? A great deal. The evangelical heritage has long identified itself with the hopes and promises of America. Evangelicals view themselves as having helped to create and sustain all that is good in America: its traditions of moral virtue; its ethic of work, commitment, and achievement; and its political and economic institutions. Conservative Protestantism has helped to define America, at least in its mythic dimensions. It is hardly surprising, then, that conservative Protestantism has defined its political interests in terms of the defense and advancement of U.S. hegemony. In so doing, evangelicals have defended and advanced their own interests as religious people.

But what of the present? The most common perception, certainly among secular cultural elites, is that conservative Protestantism continues in its traditional role, and does so more or less uniformly. This is a plausible description. Evangelicalism's loss of cultural hegemony would be less obvious if it continued to identify with the myth of America. But are these in fact the opinions of evangelicals today?

Neither the laity nor leadership is uniformly conservative on any political issue, including foreign policy. It is true that evangelicals as a whole are more conservative than most major U.S. religious groupings. Nevertheless, there are differences of opinion.

The evangelical leadership is charged with moral authority and the responsibility to express community interests. Its opinions on foreign policy issues are extremely important. Yet one immediately sees that among these leaders, there is considerable diversity.

Evangelical Elites

On the crucial issue of elite *evaluation of American hegemony,* surveys (particularly the Roper-IEA survey of American theologians) have uncovered data relevant to this discussion.[4] Asked, for example, whether they thought the United States was in general a force for good or ill in the world, 72 percent of the evangelical theologians responded "good." A similar pattern appears when the question is more specific. Asked which was the greater problem in the world today, repressive regimes aligned with the United States or Communist expansion, three-fourths chose the latter. However, when asked whether they felt we as a nation generally treated people in the Third World fairly or unfairly, nearly half (44 percent) responded "unfairly." Asked whether they thought U.S. multinational corporations help or hurt in the Third World, 48 percent said that they hurt.

A second and related category of questions deals with the *defense of American hegemony.* Half of all evangelical theologians maintained that the United States is currently spending too much for this purpose. Two recent national surveys of evangelical seminarians and college professors revealed a similar division. Sustaining American interests also raises the question of U.S. allies. Only 4 percent of the conservative Protestant theologians believed that the United States should increase the number of American troops in Europe as part of the NATO commitment. One-fourth believed that troop levels should be reduced, while 71 percent maintained that troop levels should be kept as they are.

Israel provides another divisive issue for evangelicals. Its eschatological significance for most evangelicals hardly needs mentioning. Its strategic significance to U.S. foreign policy is also obvious. For both of these reasons, Israel has long been supported by the evangelical laity. Yet on this issue, evangelical elites are sharply divided. Questioned whether America should do everything it can to support Israel, 38 percent of all evangelical seminarians agreed, 31 percent disagreed, and 30 percent were neutral. And when American theologians were asked about U.S. arms sales and military aid to anti-Communist countries, one-third thought these practices should be reduced, one-half thought levels should remain as they are now, and one-sixth approved of increases.

An important factor in all these issues is the Soviet Union. Since the 1920s, American evangelicals have felt a deep revulsion toward Communist ideologies, movements, and regimes. There was, of course, a fundamentalist link to the Brown Scare in the 1930s and a fundamentalist presence in the Red Scare in the 1950s. And suspicion of Communism continues to the present. Nearly four out of ten evangelical seminarians surveyed believed that "Communism is still a serious threat within our country." Obviously, this has practical consequences for views on American-Soviet relations: 69 percent of the seminarians believed it important that the United States maintain *at least* a balance of power with the Soviet Union; only 17 percent claimed it was not. And 61 percent favored negotiating an arms control agreement with the Soviets.

Perhaps the most interesting aspect of the evangelical elite's view of this issue is the difference of opinion on the nature of American-Soviet competition. Is it fundamentally a moral struggle between right and wrong, or even between the forces of good and evil? Or is it basically a case of power politics—a purely secular confrontation with little if any religious meaning? One might expect that evangelicals would view it as a moral struggle, because America is presumably Christian and good. For the laity, this is generally true. But for evangelical elites, the picture is different. In fact, two-thirds viewed the competition as power politics and only one-third as a moral conflict.

Ideological Division

Exploring the empirical data more carefully might be helpful, but it might also risk missing their broader significance. Even after this cursory review of elite opinion, it is fair to say that the foreign policy debate in evangelical groups centers around certain questions about the nature of America's role and evangelicalism's relationship to it. If there ever was consensus on these issues, there certainly is no consensus now. Fairly clear divisions exist, and they lead to more elaborate ideological divisions, which are intensifying somewhat.

The majority of the evangelical elite continues to be right of center. Both in political self-identification and in their opinions, close to half could be called conservative. This, of course, is only a rough approximation. Moderates make up to 30 to 40 percent and those left of center account for 15 to 25 percent. The conservatives within the evangelical leadership are often not consciously political. For a good many, political conservatism is simply part of being Christian. Only 11 percent claim to be neo-conservative and nearly a third were not even familiar with the term.

By and large, evangelicals still cling to a view of America as a great country set apart by its moral and political traditions. Few would maintain that America is really a Christian nation—the new Israel, an exemplar to all the nations. Yet neither would they say that the American moral and political heritage lacks spiritual meaning. Given the standards of good and evil established by general revelation, America, on balance, stands out as a *good*. As such it carries a moral, if not divine, responsibility to extend goodness in the world and to restrain evil.

At the opposite end of the political spectrum lies the evangelical left-liberal contingent. They view American hegemony in far less favorable terms. I believe their posture is born at least partly out of a disproportionate emphasis on the "principalities and powers" motif in the Scriptures. Taken by itself, this motif lumps together all secular institutions and authority in opposition to the Kingdom of God. By this standard, the Soviet Union and the United States are not very different. Within the principalities and powers motif, *implicit moral equivalence of nations becomes theological reality*. The principalities and powers motif has implications for Christian identity too. True Christian identity (collective or individual) cannot be discovered *within* particularistic loyalties (that is, as a loyal member of a community, region, or nation), for these are all part of the realm of darkness. True Christian identity requires exclusive loyalty to the coming kingdom. The fires of devotion to country do not burn very brightly on the evangelical Left. Indeed, quite the opposite. Analyses of evangelical Left publications reveal widespread disdain for American policies and institutions.

The evangelical Left is a sizeable minority and has grown considerably since the early 1970s. As a whole, Left evangelicals are more self-conscious about their political commitments and more politicized, and they are decidedly vocal. After all, they are political-cultural dissenters and mobilization is essential to establishing a beachhead. In any event, they appear to be much more powerful than their numbers suggest. Moreover, if there is a political drift among evangelical elites, it is generally from the Right to the Left.

PLURALISM AND THE POTENTIAL TO SHAPE FOREIGN POLICY

The current splits within evangelicalism raise an important question. What accounts for these divisions? More to the point, do neo- or paleo-conservative evangelicals come to their positions wholly out of prayerful contemplation of the issues? Or have members of the evangelical Left achieved "discernment" from spiritual experience? Other factors might be at work. We have to allow for the possibility of the spiritual having a role in all this. Yet as a sociologist, I would argue that the more profane realities of everyday life provide a more credible explanation.

The order of society is supported by an order of consciousness—symbols collectively accepted. Prior to the twentieth century, the symbolic order in America was predominantly Judeo-Christian, but more accurately, it was theologically conservative

Protestantism. The loss of Protestant hegemony was both caused by and has contributed to an intensifying moral pluralism in American society. Pluralism, whatever else it is, entails a competition to define reality. To say that pluralism is intensifying in American society is to say (among other things) not only that competition intensifies *among* different social groups but that competition is intensified *within* social groups.

This is precisely what I believe is happening within evangelical culture in the United States. With its loss of cultural hegemony, the old guard within evangelicalism has to compete not only with extrinsic religious and secular factions, but with factions within its own ranks.

The sociological solution is the formation of coalitions with social groups that share similar interests. Various factions on the Christian Right, for example, find themselves aligned with the institutions and elites of the economic establishment—the old business classes. Various factions of the evangelical Left have become aligned with the elites of the secular cultural establishment—the knowledge class or new class, as social scientists call it. (Ironically, not only is the evangelical Right aligned with "the principalities and powers," but so is the evangelical Left.)

On both sides, there are substantive differences between the evangelicals and those with whom they are aligned. The notable difference on the Left is over abortion. For paleo-conservatives, differences crop up over the priorities of the conservative agenda. (Some want to emphasize moral issues while others want to emphasize economics and defense.) All in all, though, the alliances are congenial and useful. All factions gain power and resources in their efforts to redefine social, economic, and political reality. None of this involves conspiracy, nor should the sincerity of those involved be questioned.

What does this mean for the role of evangelicals in shaping foreign policy? It means that presently they speak with several, contradictory, voices. Consequently, evangelicals do little more than add to the disorder in the public square by increasing the volume and pitch of a moral debate largely started by others. Their contributions to the debate are limited, mainly because of close political alliances and strict pursuit of specific public policies. The *Moral Majority Report*'s support of current policies in South Africa or *Sojourners'* critiques of U.S. policy in Central America are prime examples.

In my view, all evangelicals concerned with foreign policy must first struggle to find some minimal *consensus on the religious and moral meaning of America's role in the world*. In addition, evangelicals must reach *consensus over their collective identity vis-a-vis American civilization*. Consensus over specific foreign policy issues would be much more likely once these more fundamental concerns are settled.

Needless to say this will require historical, theological, political, and philosophical debates. It will also require evangelicals of all types to be more prudent about their direct or indirect alliances and about identifying too closely with any particular position. Political detachment and intense inquiry are essential because the stakes are so high. Evangelicals will be neither consistent nor effective over the long term unless they find minimal consensus among themselves.

Notes

CHAPTER ONE

1. Richard John Neuhaus, *The Naked Public Square: Religion and Democracy in America* (Grand Rapids: Eerdmans, 1984).
2. The argument in favor of the necessary, but not sufficient, role of capitalism in democratic governance is most persuasively advanced by Peter Berger in *The Capitalist Revolution* (New York: Basic, 1986).
3. For representative reading, see George Lindbeck, *The Nature of Doctrine* (Philadelphia: Westminster, 1984); and Alasdair MacIntyre, *After Virtue,* 2nd ed. (Notre Dame: University of Notre Dame Press, 1984). Of John Howard Yoder's many publications, perhaps the most powerful statement of his basic position is still *The Politics of Jesus* (Grand Rapids: Eerdmans, 1972). Of Stanley Hauerwas' prolific output, I look especially at *The Peaceable Kingdom* (Notre Dame: University of Notre Dame Press, 1983) and at an unpublished paper of 1985, "A Christian Critique of Christian America," delivered at the American Society for Political and Legal Philosophy. Unless otherwise noted, the Hauerwas quotations are from that paper. I should mention that Hauerwas and Lindbeck are close friends and have been colleagues in many projects. I am deeply indebted to them for years of intense personal conversation about some of these matters. I have no doubt the conversation will continue.
4. Hauerwas, *Peaceable Kingdom,* p. 168.
5. Ibid., p. 106.
6. Ibid., p. 23.
7. Douglas W. Frank, *Less Than Conquerors: How Evangelicals Entered the Twentieth Century* (Grand Rapids: Eerdmans, 1986). For a more thorough analysis of Frank's argument, see Richard John Neuhaus, "Christian Monisms Against the Gospel," *Religion and Society Report,* November 1987.
8. Ronald J. Sider, "Towards a Political Philosophy," *ESA Advocate,* October 1988.
9. For the suggestion of Augustine rather than Benedict, I am indebted to Gilbert Meilaender of Oberlin College.

CHAPTER TWO

1. Some of the best-known figures within the broad intellectual movement known as "the radical evangelicals" include Nicholas Wolterstorff, Ronald

Sider, and Jim Wallis. For representative works, see Wolterstorff, *Until Justice and Peace Embrace* (Grand Rapids: Eerdmans, 1983); Wallis, *Agenda for Biblical People,* 2nd ed. (New York: Harper & Row, 1984); Sider, *Rich Christians in an Age of Hunger,* 2nd ed. (Madison: Inter-Varsity Press, 1984).

2. The *Political Writings of St. Augustine,* ed. Henry Paolucci (South Bend: Regnery Gateway, 1962); Blaise Pascal, *Pensees,* trans. W. F. Trotter (New York: Dutton, 1958), nos. 1, 73, 82, 83, 99, 100, 116, 131, 139, 142, 176, 267, 272, 294, 295, 296, 298, 299, 301, 311, 320, 331, 334, 358, 375, 402, 422, 424, 453, 456, 472, 477, 555; Reinhold Niebuhr, *The Nature and Destiny of Man* (New York: Scribner's, 1943).

3. Thomas Hobbes, *Leviathan,* ed. Michael Oakeshott (New York: Collier, 1968), esp. ch. 11 ("Of the Difference of Manners") and ch. 13 ("Of the Natural Condition of Mankind as Concerning their Felicity and Misery"); Niccolo Machiavelli, *The Prince,* trans. and ed. T. G. Bergin (Northbrook, Ill.: AHM Pub., 1947). Thrasymachus defined justice as "nothing other than the advantage of the stronger"; see Plato, *The Republic,* I, 338c. See also the speech by the Athenian generals to the magistrates of the island city-state of Melos: "You know as well as we do that, when these matters are discussed by practical people, the standard of justice depends on the equality of power to compel and that in fact the strong do what they have the power to do and the weak accept what they have to accept" (V, 89). I would distinguish this form of secular realism not only from Christian realism, but also from the twentieth-century school of such "political realists" as Hans Morgenthau and George Kennan. In spite of ambiguities at some points in their writings, both these writers acknowledge the existence of moral absolutes and the validity of some moral restraints on the pursuit of power politics.

4. Leo Strauss, *Thoughts on Machiavelli* (Glencoe, Ill.: The Free Press, 1958).

5. E. B. F. Midgley, *The Natural Law Tradition and the Theory of International Relations* (London: Elek Books, 1975). In fairness, it must be pointed out that some of the later Christian realists such as Pascal have been downright skeptical of natural law, while others such as Niebuhr have focused on its limitations.

6. This perspective has been best expressed by the non-Christian philosopher of international politics, Raymond Aron, and his notion of the "indeterminacy of international relations." See Aron, *Peace and War* (Garden City: Doubleday, 1966).

7. Charles W. Kegley, "Neo-Idealism: A Practical Matter," *Ethics and International Affairs,* 2 (1988), 173–197.

8. For the failure of appeasement, see Williamson Murray, *The Change in the European Balance of Power, 1938–1939: The Path to Ruin* (Princeton: Princeton University Press, 1984); concerning Cortez's conquest of the Aztec kingdoms, see Bernal Diaz del Castillo, *Historia Verdadera de la Conquista de la Neuva Espana* (Madrid, 1933). For other conquerors and highly ambitious leaders, see the accounts of Genghis Khan and Timur in Edward Gibbon, *History of the Decline and Fall of the Roman Empire* (New York: Modern Library, n.d.), chs. 64–65; of Alexander the Great in Arrian, *The Campaigns of Alexander* (London: Penguin Books, 1981); of Julius Caesar in Plutarch, *The Lives of the Noble Grecians and Romans,* trans. John Dryden (New York:

Modern Library, n.d.); of Frederick the Great in Gerhard Ritter, *Frederick the Great* (Berkeley: University of California Press, 1968); of Peter the Great in Robert K. Massie, *Peter the Great* (New York: Ballantine Books, 1980); and of Napoleon Bonaparte in Felix Markham, *Napoleon* (New York: New American Library, 1963).

9. This is one of the key themes in Paul Kennedy, *The Rise and Fall of the Great Powers* (New York: Random House, 1988). It is unfortunate that Kennedy extends his admirably well-researched historical argument to support a less obvious but highly fashionable conclusion: that the United States in the 1980s is about to join the list of once great powers in decline as a result of its own "imperial overstretch." For a convincing refutation of this aspect of Kennedy's thesis, see Joseph S. Nye, Jr., "Understanding U.S. Strength," *Foreign Policy,* 72 (Fall 1988), 105–129.

10. Matt. 3:2.

11. James 2:5.

12. From this perspective, therefore, the ethics of the Sermon are best brought into the political world as "reminders" that statesmen should keep in the back of their minds as they formulate political strategies and, when the circumstances warrant, as principles that help shape the general guidelines for particular policies. To see them instead as a set of rules that can be mechanically translated into all circumstances is highly problematical. It runs the danger, in the words of Oxford philosopher G. E. M. Anscombe, of turning Christianity from "a severe and practical religion . . . [into] a beautifully ideal but impracticable one." Anscombe's trenchant theological critique of pacifism is contained in her essay "War and Murder" in *Nuclear Weapons and Christian Conscience,* ed. Walter Stein (London: Merlin Press, 1965), p. 53.

13. Herbert Deane, *The Political and Social Ideas of St. Augustine* (New York: Columbia University Press, 1963).

14. *Lord Acton: Essays on Freedom and Power,* ed. Gertrude Himmelfarb (Boston: Beacon Press, 1948).

15. Jacob Burckhardt, *Reflections on History* (Indianapolis: Liberty Classics, 1979), pp. 332–333.

16. Kenneth N. Waltz, *Man, the State, and War* (New York: Columbia University Press, 1959).

17. Michael Howard, *The Causes of Wars* (Cambridge: Harvard University Press, 1983), pp. 49–64.

18. Cited in Alberto R. Coll, *The Wisdom of Statecraft* (Durham: Duke University Press, 1985), p. 94.

19. This view was best articulated by the nineteenth-century German historian Leopold von Ranke in his essays "The Great Powers" and "A Dialogue on Politics." See von Ranke, *The Theory and Practice of History,* ed. Iggers and von Moltke (New York: Bobbs-Merrill, 1973).

20. Adda B. Bozeman, *Politics and Culture in International History* (Princeton: Princeton University Press, 1960), and *The Future of Law in a Multicultural World* (Princeton: Princeton University Press, 1971).

21. Kenneth W. Thompson, *Morality and Foreign Policy* (Baton Rouge. Louisiana State University Press, 1980), pp. 162–174.

22. Several useful antidotes to the radical evangelicals' tendencies in this regard are Bozeman, *Politics and Culture;* Robert W. Tucker, *The Inequality*

of Nations (New York: Basic Books, 1977); P. T. Bauer, *Equality, the Third World, and Economic Delusion* (Cambridge: Harvard University Press, 1981); Lawrence Harrison, *Underdevelopment as a State of Mind* (Lanham, Md.: University Press of America, 1984); and the critiques of "tercermundismo" ("Thirdworldism") by the Venezuelan writer Carlos Rangel and the French essayist Jean-François Revel.

23. See G. R. Dunstan, "Theological Method in the Deterrence Debate," and Arthur Hockaday, "In Defense of Deterrence," in *Ethics and Nuclear Deterrence,* ed. Geoffrey Goodwin (New York: St. Martin's Press, 1982), pp. 40–51, 68–93. The case *against* the acceptability of nuclear deterrence has been elaborated most powerfully by non-pacifist, conservative Roman Catholic philosophers such as Anscombe, "War and Murder," pp. 45–62; and John Finnis, Joseph M. Boyle, Jr., and Germain Grisez, *Nuclear Deterrence, Morality, and Realism* (New York: Oxford University Press, 1987).

24. Carthage's destruction by Rome in 146 B.C. provides an excellent example of the perils of unilateral disarmament. See the haunting account in *Polybius on Roman Imperialism: The Histories of Polybius,* translated from the text of H. Hultsch by Evelyn S. Shuckburgh, abridged with an introduction by Alvin H. Bernstein (South Bend: Regnery Gateway, 1980).

25. Aristotle, *Nicomachean Ethics,* VI.

26. Thompson, *Morality,* p. 139.

27. Joseph Pieper, *The Four Cardinal Virtues* (Notre Dame: University of Notre Dame Press, 1966), p. 7.

28. Ibid., pp. 14–18.

29. Ibid., p. 21.

30. Thomas Aquinas, *Summa Theologica,* I–II, Q. 57, art. 4. Aquinas also pointed out that "some men, in so far as they are good counsellors in matters of warfare, or seamanship, are said to be prudent officers or pilots, but not prudent absolutely; for only those are prudent absolutely who give good counsel about what concerns man's entire life" (ibid.).

31. Pieper, *Four Cardinal Virtues,* p. 25.

32. Winston S. Churchill, *The Gathering Storm* (Boston: Houghton Mifflin, 1948), p. 320.

33. Pieper, *Four Cardinal Virtues,* pp. 27–28.

34. See the discussion in Clark E. Cochran, "The Radical Gospel and Christian Prudence," in *The Ethical Dimension of Political Life: Essays in Honor of John H. Hallowell,* ed. Francis Canavan (Durham: Duke University Press, 1983), pp. 188–199.

35. Winston S. Churchill, *Closing the Ring* (Boston: Houghton Mifflin, 1951), pp. 373–374.

36. See the account in J. E. Hare and Carey B. Joynt, *Ethics and International Affairs* (New York: St. Martin's Press, 1982), pp. 90–94.

37. Reinhold Niebuhr, *Moral Man and Immoral Society* (New York: Scribner's, 1960), pp. 83–112.

38. *New Catholic Encyclopedia* (New York: McGraw-Hill, 1967), 11:928, col. 2, cited in Cochran, "Radical Gospel," p. 196.

39. Eric Voegelin, *Order and History,* vol. IV: *The Ecumenic Age* (Baton Rouge: Louisiana State University Press, 1974).

40. Bismarck is characterized as a shrewd, yet basically prudent statesman

by A. J. P. Taylor, *Bismarck: The Man and the Statesman* (New York: Random House, 1967). Cf. Edward Crankshaw, *Bismarck* (London: Penguin Books, 1983).

41. In Bismarck's own time there were a few prescient souls aware of the hidden long-term costs of the Bismarckian enterprise. Crown Prince Frederick of Prussia remarked on December 31, 1870, "Bismarck has made us great and powerful, but he has robbed us of our friends, the sympathies of the world, and—our conscience." And Jacob Burckhardt, the Swiss historian who towards the end of the nineteenth century foresaw the coming of a new age of global wars and dictatorships, observed in one of his lectures in 1871: "Oh how the German nation errs if it thinks it will be able to put the rifle in one corner and turn to the arts and the happiness of peace! They will be told above all you must continue your military training! And after a time no one will really be able to say what is the purpose of living. For soon the German-Russian war will loom on the horizon." Quoted in Crankshaw, *Bismarck*, p. 301.

42. See the fascinating debate in Hans Kohn, *German History: Some New German Views* (Boston: Beacon Press, 1954), which contains an agonizing reappraisal of the Bismarckian legacy in the light of Germany's fate in the aftermath of World War II.

43. Reinhold Niebuhr, *The Children of Light and the Children of Darkness* (New York: Scribner's, 1944), p. 189.

44. "The Christian Gospel will be most effective in this political context in the character which it imprints upon Christian men carrying responsibility in the relevant exercise of judgement and use of power—notably in the gifts of penitent self-knowledge, humility, patience, courage, and, perhaps above all, prudence. 'A right judgment in all things' is the substance of an ancient Christian prayer, and, indeed, of a Dominical promise" (Dunstan, "Theological Method," p. 51).

CHAPTER THREE

1. The terms "fundamentalism" and "evangelicalism" have in the past been used to differentiate between the historical and sociological variations of theologically conservative Christianity in America. However, in recent years it has been the convention to use the term "evangelical" to describe *all* theologically conservative Christians. Throughout this paper I use the terms "evangelical" and "evangelicalism" to refer to those people, institutions, organizations, and movements that are associated with theologically conservative Christianity.

2. The question of why evangelicalism redefined itself is interesting and complex. Certainly many within the evangelical world argue that this theological redefinition was the result of a more accurate reading of the Bible. This may indeed be partly true; however, it is also clear that the social pressures of modernity cannot be discounted as a force influencing the development of evangelical theology. This point is made eloquently in James Davison Hunter's *American Evangelicalism: Conservative Religion and the Quandary of Modernity* (New Brunswick: Rutgers University Press, 1983) and *Evangelicalism: The Coming Generation* (Chicago: University of Chicago Press, 1987).

3. Thomas D. Ice and H. Wayne House have recently written the first

substantive history and critique of Christian Reconstructionism; see *Dominion Theology: Blessing Or Curse?* (Portland: Multnomah Press, 1988). Ice and House are both affiliated with Dallas Theological Seminary, an institution associated with the fundamentalist wing of American evangelicalism. Interestingly, Dallas has been in the forefront of the evangelical critique of Reconstructionist theology.

4. See Ice and House, *Dominion Theology*, pp. 367–395.

5. James W. Skillen, "Public Justice and True Tolerance," in *Confessing Christ and Doing Politics*, ed. Skillen (Washington: Association for Public Justice Education Fund, 1982), p. 56.

6. Ibid., p. 54.

7. Stephen Monsma, *Pursuing Justice in a Sinful World* (Grand Rapids: Eerdmans, 1984), p. 7.

8. James W. Skillen, *Christians Organizing for Political Service* (Washington: Association for Public Justice Education Fund, 1980), p. 17.

9. Monsma, *Pursuing Justice*, p. 4.

10. James W. Skillen, "The Bible, Politics, and Democracy: What Does Biblical Obedience Entail for American Political Thought," in *The Bible, Politics, and Democracy*, ed. Richard John Neuhaus (Grand Rapids: Eerdmans, 1987), pp. 58, 61, 80, 62, 67.

11. Skillen, *Confessing Christ*, pp. 61, 60.

12. Clark Pinnock, "A Pilgrimage in Political Theology," in *On Liberation Theology*, ed. Ronald H. Nash (Milford, Mich.: Mott Media, 1984), p. 109.

13. Richard Mouw, *Politics and the Biblical Drama* (Grand Rapids: Eerdmans, 1976), p. 116.

14. Stanley Hauerwas, *Against the Nations: War and Survival in a Liberal Society* (Minneapolis: Winston Press, 1985), p. 130.

15. An exhaustive treatment of this subject is Bruce Demarest's *General Revelation: Historical Views and Contemporary Issues* (Grand Rapids: Zondervan, 1982).

16. Ibid., p. 14.

17. Ernest L. Fortin, "St. Thomas Aquinas," in *History of Political Philosophy*, ed. Leo Strauss and Joseph Cropsey (Chicago: University of Chicago Press, 1981), p. 227.

18. Indeed, the primacy of faith and special revelation in matters of faith was what the Reformation was all about. The principles of *sola fide, sola gratia,* and *sola Scriptura* were central to the Reformation movement. See Demarest, *General Revelation*, p. 42.

19. See Arvin Vos, *Aquinas and Calvin and Contemporary Protestant Thought* (Grand Rapids: Eerdmans, 1985).

20. In a very important sense, theological liberalism, as it emerged in the late eighteenth and early nineteenth centuries, was a romantic reaction against rationalism. However, both rejected the classic Christian belief in a supernatural special revelation.

21. Cornelius Van Til, *In Defense of the Faith*, 3rd ed. (Phillipsburg, N.J.: The Presbyterian and Reformed Publishing Company, 1967), p. 44.

22. Quoted in R. J. Rushdoony, *The Word of Flux* (Fairfax, Va.: Thoburn Press, 1975), p. 89.

23. Van Til, *Defense of the Faith*, p. 77.

24. Rushdoony, *Word of Flux,* p. 79.

25. R. J. Rushdoony, *By What Standard?* (Philadelphia: The Presbyterian and Reformed Publishing Company, 1959), pp. 11, 17.

26. Ibid., p. 3; quoted in Rushdoony, *Word of Flux,* p. 90.

CHAPTER FOUR

1. Timothy Smith, "Protestant Schooling and American Nationality, 1800–1850," *Journal of American History,* 53, 4 (1967), 687.

2. Albert Bergesen and Ronald Schoenberg, "Long Waves of Colonial Expansion and Contraction, 1415–1969," in *Studies of the Modern World-System,* ed. Bergesen (New York: Academic Press, 1980).

3. Lester Thurow, "The Moral Equivalent of Defeat," *Foreign Policy,* 42 (Spring 1981), 114–124; Bergesen and Schoenberg, "Long Waves"; and Bergesen and Chintamani Sahoo, "Evidence of the Decline of American Hegemony in World Production," *Review,* 8, 4 (1985), 595–611.

4. "The IEA/Roper Center Theology Faculty Survey," *This World,* 2 (Summer 1982).

Index of Names